HE JESUS AND MARY CHAIN

MUSICAL BIOGRAPHY BY JOHN ROBERTSON

Omnibus Press
London/New York/Sydney/Cologne

Edited by *Chris Charlesworth*
Book Designed by *Laurence Stevens*
Picture Research by *Mary McCartney*
Project and typesetting co-ordinated by *Caroline Watson*

ISBN 0.7119.1470.2
Order No: OP44734

Exclusive distributors:
Book Sales Limited
8/9 Frith Street,
London W1V 5TZ, UK

Music Sales Corporation
24 East 22nd Street,
New York, NY 10010, USA

Music Sales Pty Limited
120 Rothschild Avenue,
Rosebery, NSW 2018, Australia

To the Music Trade only:
Music Sales Limited,
8/9 Frith Street,
London W1V 5TZ, UK

Picture credits
Peter Anderson Front and Back Covers, p4, 6, 12, 23, 37, 38, 41, 46, 52,
53, 72, 74, 77, 89, 94 **John Blackmore** p90 **Blanco Y Negro** p40, 83, 88
Andrew Catlin p34, 58 **Chris Clunn** p26, 30, 32, 44, 55, 64, 67, 75, 82
Dezo Hoffmann p13, **Lesley Howling** p14, 16 **London Features Int** p8, 20,
24, 25, 54, 56, 60, 62b, 70, 81, 84, 85, 93, 95 **Gary Lornie** p86 **Music
Sales Ltd** p28, 29, 63 **Tony Mottram** p9, 19, 22, 27, 33, 42, 61, 76, 92 **Phil
Nicholls** p57, 78 **Andy Phillips** p11, 17, 18, 35, 71 **RCA** p45 **Alan Reevell**
p10, 36, 50, 68, 69 **Sheila Rock** p66, 80.

Typeset by Capital Setters, London.
Printed in England by Anchor Brendon Limited, Tiptree, Essex.

Whistle In
▶
CHAPTER 1

It began as a distant whine, something you could ignore by concentrating on the muzak from the radio alongside you. Crackling closer to the nerve, the drill becomes sharper and greedier, thrusting aside the fragile enamel defences and jetting towards the centre. As the whistle screams to a crescendo, and the anaesthetic fades, there is only the nerve, and the drill, and in the background, lost behind the piercing whine, the faintly familiar chords of a three-chord pop song. You have been listening to The Jesus And Mary Chain.

Once in a decade, a sound emerges that shatters the boundaries of popular music. As the music business grows in financial importance, and fragments into endless ghettos of cult appeal, so the impact of each new arrival is lessened. Elvis Presley and The Beatles changed the world. The Sex Pistols changed Britain. It may be the legacy of The Jesus And Mary Chain to have changed only Scotland.

No matter: their music has met the dual challenge that faces any iconoclast – it is subversive, and it is commercial. Settling for either is an easy option; achieving both takes courage, commitment and a touch of genius. The Jesus And Mary Chain are the first rock band to take the principles of the avant-garde, and apply them to commercial pop. Their weapons: noise, unrestrained power and intelligence. All three threaten a dominant culture built on unquestioning acceptance.

Multi-capitalist enterprises dominate international popular music: marketing campaigns are masterminded in Los Angeles, New York and London, and sweep the world according to plan. Rebellion can be marketed as easily as any other commodity, providing the rebels are only skin-deep. The ultimate victory is to use the tools of the establishment to undermine its own foundations; in musical terms, persuading a major record company to finance the demolition of its artistic credo. The Jesus And Mary Chain are signed to the world's biggest record company; they have hit records with music that goes against all the pre-packaged certainties of the international marketing men. They know that those who do not understand the past are condemned to repeat it, and that you have to clear the site before you can build on it.

Above all, theirs is the triumph of freedom over restriction; of action over inertia; and of noise over silence. The battle is by no means won; it may never be. Already, The Mary Chain have found that change can be as unsettling to rebels as it is to the establishment, that today's cultural heroes are tomorrow's traitors. Their future is uncertain. Their music may be a last blaze of glory before we are all synthesised into conformity, our hopes and desires sampled and tamed before we are allowed to enjoy them. Tomorrow's rebellion will be part of a Levi's commercial. For today, The Jesus And Mary Chain advertise nothing but their own ideals.

In My Room

▶

CHAPTER 2

Take the London Road out of Glasgow, 15 miles to the south-east, and you will reach East Kilbride. Scotland's first New Town was constructed on a windswept hill as an overspill area for the teeming metropolis of Glasgow, and presented a preferable option to the crowded tenements that litter the east side of the city.

Like all New Towns, East Kilbride was built on hope. The town was planned on progressive lines, with housing estates each having their local focus – community centre, church or shops. What was missing was tradition, and culture – not just art galleries and museums, but a community spirit that could give birth to authentic local voices. East Kilbride is dominated by Glasgow, but has little of its spirit. Before The Jesus And Mary Chain, its artistic credentials were nil.

The brothers who were to change East Kilbride's reputation were born in the years between the birth of rock 'n' roll and the rise of Britain's alternative, the Beat Boom – William Reid in around 1958 and James circa 1961. Both men were to claim to be in their teens when The Mary Chain recorded their first single in 1984. "It's a secret," maintained Jim Reid when the truth broke a year later. "I'm quite old but I deny it. I'm in my twenties. It's a bit of a mystery if I don't tell you. Maybe that's pretty pathetic, but I'm pretty vain."

Their childhood was, by their own account, unremarkable. There are no tales of pre-teen precocity to enliven the standard progression from one school to another, or from education to their first dead-end jobs. "I never really had that happy a childhood," Jim Reid recalled. "But I never really had that miserable a childhood. Nothing happened. I wasn't very happy, probably just because of the way I was more than anything else. I wish I could have been a bit more rebellious. I accepted too much. I disapproved of an awful lot, but I never really did anything about it. I just sat quietly and accepted everything."

In the early eighties, William and Jim first considered the idea of forming a band. Rather than playing local gigs, like most budding rebels, they stayed indoors. Jim Reid: "We were kind of weirdos. We really did spend five years without going out almost at all. We'd take the dog for a walk, or go out and sign on. We enjoyed the dole – we stayed on it for five years, though I've got to admit the last two years were pretty deadly. But the first three were the closest I've ever been to happiness.

"Admittedly we had no money, but the kind of things we'd do, we didn't need any. I'd go to places on my bicycle and occasionally I had enough money to go to the pub, and as I couldn't afford records, I'd tape them. It was quite a nice existence; there were no complications. I was living in my parents' home, and they supplied my meals and bed. I had just enough to spend on crisps and pints of beer.

"Our parents used to think we were absolutely mad! They were quite tolerant. They occasionally threatened to kick us out but they were too nice for that!" The Reids had orthodox plans for their sons, however: "They wanted me and William to get a decent job, a girlfriend, get married and go down the pub with my dad. It kind of disappointed them, because they thought we weren't ever going to amount to anything. They'd see us staying in writing and recording songs, and they just thought we were complete psychos."

Assembling material and an image, the Reids had to put up with criticism from inside and outside the home. Jim himself sometimes began to doubt the reality of what they were doing: "There was a time when I began to think it was never going anywhere. I began to lose faith. It was very terrifying. There's nothing else I can do, nothing else I'm interested in. There was no alternative. I'd got no particular interest in working in a meat packer's factory."

Or, presumably, a cheese factory, which is where teenage Jim found himself for several months before he gathered the nerve to quit. Like scores of working-class kids before them, the Reids had no chance of escape from their surroundings, except through a career that would not hold their roots against them.

Rock music, which swallowed the 'white trash' Elvis Presley, scouser Beatles and cockney Sex Pistols, was broad enough to take on two kids from East Kilbride. Jim and William had their future planned from the start: "The whole idea of The Jesus And Mary Chain was worked out between the two of us in those five years. The sound, the image: everything was worked out."

The Reids were at an ideal age to be entranced by the arrival of punk music in 1976. The origins and aims of punk have been obscured by the theoretical ravings of Malcolm McLaren, and the sociological jargon dropped by a phalanx of professional cultural observers. For McLaren, punk was just one more art school prank, the ultimate rock 'n' roll swindle. For The Sex Pistols, acknowledged musical and moral leaders of the punk scene, it was a chance to echo the sound of their chosen heroes, like The New York Dolls and The Stooges. For the sociologists, it was the cry of a wounded generation, a movement of the young and dispossessed with no future to call their own.

In retrospect, all three strains combined to produce the cultural maelstrom that shocked London in 1976 and 1977. Just as it did a decade later, the rock establishment felt it had things sewn up. Rock was growing old alongside the fans who had helped it mature in the sixties, and with the death of glam-rock a couple of years earlier there was nothing specifically teenage for kids to follow – no equivalent of the long-haired, immoral and quite probably dirty Rolling Stones, who could act as role model for the young and irritant to their elders and betters.

Punk also gave voice to the generation who suffered as the recession started to bite and unemployment to rise. But it was never a definite political movement, despite the attempts of various organisations on the left and right to make it one. Individual groups had their pet causes and slogans – boredom with the USA, anarchy closer to home, our generation being preferable to yours – but there was no common bond beyond fashion and attitude. And punks proved to be just as conservative as the hidebound hippies they wanted to replace.

A decade after anarchy was supposed to root out complacency and order, punks still roamed the streets of London, shocking only American tourists and elderly relations.

"Punk came along and made me think about things," Jim Reid remembers. Its stripped-down, three-chord, no-nonsense structure appealed to self-taught musicians, and its illusion of cultural power – plus the tribal identification that was one of its most striking qualities – inspired teenagers all over the country to take up their instruments and rebel.

At the same time, punk spawned an independent music business network, a chain of homegrown, backyard record companies that existed beyond the whim and control of the increasingly isolated major labels. The top bands did 'sell out', as the cliché of the time had it, by registering their signatures on major label contracts at the earliest opportunity. But within two years, the indie labels completely dominated the British weekly rock press, while the majors fished desperately for trends and cults to satisfy their built-in need for success. The indies were genuinely innovative; and if you couldn't find soulmates to sign you up, you simply started your own label.

By the early eighties, however, the indies were fast becoming a self-imposed ghetto. The original punk bands had disintegrated like shooting stars, sending violent sparks in all directions; or they had overcome their boredom with the USA long enough to follow in the footsteps of their original targets. Disillusionment was rife, and Jim Reid shared the general feeling: "It did nothing. Punk influenced a few people to get off their arses and start a group, but it wasn't the end of anything. It was just another fashion. Half the '77 punk bands were naïve, and the other half were lying bastards. I was young at the time and I believed in the whole thing. It influenced me to make music. But if ever I was doing it purely to make money, I think I'd have to stop doing interviews and speaking to people."

The Reids believed in the dream, if not in the sincerity of the punk revolution. The early eighties presented another possible role model, in the shape of a Scottish musical renaissance – centred around Alan Horne's Postcard label.

Postcard became a cult, and the cult survives today. It was remarkable not so much for its music, though the label did issue some wonderful records, as for its lack of compromise. In the past, Scottish music had been ignored by the London music industry. Scottish talent always had to come south. Alex Harvey was billed as 'The Scottish Tommy Steele' in the late fifties, yet he far outshone the 'Little White Bull' merchant in terms of rock 'n' roll authenticity. But despite recording regularly throughout the sixties, he made no commercial impact outside Scotland until the early seventies, when he was based in London. Other Scottish rockers shared an even more ignominious fate, rarely recording at all.

During the sixties beat boom, Glasgow and Edinburgh were eventually raided by talent scouts when all possible English cities had been stripped of their beat groups. In particular, Decca signed a clutch of top Scottish bands, notably The Poets, one of the most ambitious outfits to record in Britain in the sixties. But the London labels insisted that The Poets, and their contemporaries, move south. Some refused, and were resigned to the ill-distributed Scottish indie network. Others came to London, and promptly lost contact with their roots. In extreme cases, A&R men transformed Scottish bands into teenybop pop stars, giving Marmalade and The Bay City Rollers a taste of fame, but juicing Scotland of its talent.

Glasgow has always been a soul town, right from the late fifties. More than any other city, it deserves the title of Britain's white soul capital. The tradition survives today, in bands like Deacon Blue, Danny Wilson and Wet Wet Wet. A second musical current is also deeply rooted in Scotland, however – the garage band.

It was this tradition that inspired the Postcard label, though the soul culture also left its mark. Alan Horne groomed a school of young, sometimes school-age bands, all of whom had shared influences – The Velvet Underground, British psychedelia, The Buzzcocks and the lush American romanticism of Arthur Lee's Love. The label was launched with Orange Juice's 'Falling And Laughing'; later Postcard releases included the same band's obvious Velvets tribute, 'Blue Boy', two sublime singles by Roddy Frame's Aztec Camera, and a bunch of singles (and Postcard's only album) by the grimmer, less melodic Josef K.

Jim Reid claims to despise the Postcard set-up – "The whole Scottish scene turns our stomachs," he commented early in 1985 – though it was probably more the media image of Scotland that Postcard inspired which drew his ire. "The Scottish music scene has been trying to wring that neck ever since," he complained when The Mary Chain's first single was released, "And they're so dumb they don't realise that to succeed again they've got to do something different." Something different was precisely what The Jesus And Mary Chain were preparing to unleash.

THE HISTORY
of **FEEDBACK**
PART ①

" 'I Feel Fine' – that's me completely. Including the electric guitar lick and the record with the first feedback anywhere. I defy anybody to find a record – unless it's some old blues record from 1922 – that uses feedback that way. So I claim it for The Beatles. Before Hendrix, before The Who, before anybody. The first feedback on any record." (John Lennon, 1980.)

With their matching stage suits and choreographed bows after every song, The Beatles might seem unlikely precursors of The Jesus And Mary Chain. In October 1964, however, they recorded their eighth single, and seventh straight number one, 'I Feel Fine'. The record began with the heavy thump of plectrum against bass string, followed by a growling buzz of feedback, before Lennon and Harrison locked guitars into the intricate riff that underpinned the song. EMI issued the record with a public warning that the bizarre noise was deliberate, not a pressing fault – though they claimed that the feedback had been accidental. Not so: the original session tapes reveal The Beatles experimenting with the howl of feedback on take after take, until the moulding of noise and melody was achieved to their satisfaction.

The Beatles had more far-reaching ambitions than the harnessing of noise, and their initial foray into feedback was ignored in the studio for four years. In 1968, during the recording of the 'White Album', Paul McCartney unleashed a proto-metal extravaganza called 'Helter Skelter', which married apocalyptic lyrics to a steamroller guitar riff. The song climaxed in a cascade of feedback fragments, diamond shards of noise that sliced through the meat of the rhythm section. For a few seconds, there was chaos – horns, explosions, rockets, screams – before the riff re-established hold and rode the squealing white noise into the ground. Hardcore? Heavy metal? Ask Charles Manson.

Heroes And Villains
▶
CHAPTER 3

"Glasgow never accepted us; we couldn't even get played. They didn't want anything to do with us. We would take our tapes around and people would laugh at us. That's why we had to come to London."
(Jim Reid, February 1985)

Throughout 1983, William and Jim Reid recorded two-man demos at their home in East Kilbride. These were sent out to local record companies, using names like The Poppy Seeds. 'Something's Wrong', 'Inside Me', 'In A Hole', 'It's So Hard', and 'Just Out Of Reach' were among the songs premièred at this stage. All of them were rejected. "When we made our first demo tape, it did sound a bit like The Ramones," William recalled. "That's why we started using noise and feedback. We want to make records that sound different. What's the point in reviving old styles?"

The Ramones were the nearest American equivalent to The Sex Pistols, comic-book New York punks gangling in leather jackets and blue jeans. They churned out identical 90-second blasts of rock 'n' roll, with deliberately 'dumb' lyrics and three-chord structures. Their inspirations? Early sixties US rock, from the girl groups to surf music – the classic soundtracks to teenage life and beach movies. Their imagery was updated; Sheena was now a punk rocker, not a surfer girl; but their trash aesthetic retained the innocence of California pop, coated with the knowingness of New York City street life.

The Reids shared these influences, though the passage of another decade had refined them still further. "The nearest thing to a perfect record is 'The Leader Of The Pack' by the Shangri-Las," claimed William in 1985, forgetting his previous claims for The Velvets and The Stooges. The Shangri-Las were a model worth following. This four-piece white girl group from Queens, New York, cut a remarkable series of teenage soap operas translated into three-minute pop classics. Their records were masterminded by producer George 'Shadow' Morton, who lived up to the characters in his songs. In 'Leader Of The Pack', a motorbike gang leader rides to his death with the nasal tones of his girl still ringing in his ears. 'I Can Never Go Home Anymore' found the girl regretting the generation gap that estranged her from her mother, who has just died. And in 'Past, Present And Future', she recites a strange series of non-sequiturs about love, loss and sexual frigidity while the orchestra plays Beethoven's 'Moonlight Sonata'.

What makes these records great, gives them the power to reach beyond Queens to East Kilbride, is their sincerity. They are massively contrived, hopelessly over-arranged; but they shine with honesty. In the Shangri-Las, Morton found ideal soap opera queens, able to turn from triumph to tears in the course of a single line. The combination of teenage angst, remarkable sound effects (motorbikes, waves crashing on the beach, the band at the high school prom), and the kitschy between-verse dialogue makes them utterly irresistible.

"We all love the Shangri-Las, and one day we're going to make Shangri-Las records."
(Jim Reid, March 1985.)

By early 1984, the Reids – with young bassist Douglas Hart and drummer Murray Dalglish – were ready to perform in public. At around this time, they hit upon a name: The Jesus And Mary Chain. They later told fanzine journalists that the line came from a Bing Crosby movie; and then denied this six months later. William Reid explained: "The name doesn't mean anything. It was just that we needed a name in a hurry, and it was the best one we'd written down on the list. But it's a name that sticks in the mind when you've heard it, and we're going to make sure no-one forgets it."

After exhaustive rehearsals, the J&MC began to gig around East Kilbride, and then in Glasgow, in the spring of 1984. Jim Reid handled the deadpan vocals; brother William added feedback guitar and power chords. Douglas Hart made the best of his three-string bass, while drummer Murray Dalglish thumped hell out of his two-piece kit. The noise they made was incoherent, frightening, hellish, and few promoters asked for a return engagement. The Mary Chain took to gatecrashing gigs pretending to be the support band, howling through their 20-minute set and making a quick exit. "When we started the group, we knew what we were," Jim remembers. "We all really believed we were brilliant. But we didn't think anybody would listen because we were so noisy. We didn't sound like anybody else and we were rejected everywhere. I was surprised when we first ever got a gig. And after that, I started to think that anything could happen, anything at all."

Scotland offered few opportunities for career advancement, however. The Glasgow music aristocracy laughed at the band, as much for their concentration on American garage band influences as for their piercing feedback. "We had the sound we wanted, and we had the ideas," Jim said later that year, "but we realised that to succeed we had to get out of Glasgow, because musically the place is an absolute shithole. There are so many crap bands, and yet there are so many ways in which they could improve if they had the right attitude."

In May 1984, the band moved to London, taking a grubby bedsit in Fulham, surrounded by the assorted alcoholics, drug addicts and Australian students who haunt this area of West London. There they came across Alan McGee, a Scot like themselves, who was running an independent label called Creation Records, and a tiny backroom venue called The Living Room.

"I was just pissed off with music, so to entertain myself, I decided to put on a few groups." So McGee opened The Living Room to the likes of Joe Foster's Television Personalities, and The Singing Nightingales. Similarly-minded bands flocked to add their name to his date sheet, and McGee was soon promoting several shows a week. The next step was the label, which was launched with a single by The Legend – fanzine editor, *NME* journalist and idiosyncratic recording artist. The first Creation record ran to just 100 copies, and now sells for an earl's ransom on the collector's market. More singles followed, with more substantial pressings. Among the artistes on the label were The Pastels, one of many young bands who wore their admiration for The Velvet Underground openly on their sleeves; and the Pop-Art inspired Biff! Bang! Pow!

The Mary Chain made their début at The Living Room on June 9, 1984. "Obviously, no-one had come to see us," Jim recalled, "and most of them just looked astonished. About a dozen people really liked it. Next time, it was two dozen, and it grew and grew." Among the dozen who heard the melodies through the feedback was Alan McGee. He offered the band an instant one-off deal on the strength of their soundcheck before the gig.

During October, the recording session finally took place. The band taped their own 'Upside Down', and a cover of 'Vegetable Man' by Syd Barrett of Pink Floyd, with Joe Foster at the controls. McGee claimed he had to go in the following night and perform a radical remix on Foster's sub-standard work. On the record, McGee took credit for the A-side, and gave Foster the title of producer for the flip. Either way, The Jesus And Mary Chain's first record was issued in the first week of November, 1984.

It was a stunning début. Quite simply, 'Upside Down' was one of the most revolutionary records in rock history. It opened with Dalglish's bass and snare, swathed in echo – and then the screech of William Reid's feedback guitar, cutting like an industrial lathe through metal. The song was simple and repetitive, all hooks and choruses; and beneath it lay three layers of guitar, a Pistols-style rhythm thrash buried beneath high and low feedback. Jim Reid's lyrics summed up the record perfectly: 'I heard that ringing sound . . . felt I was going mad . . . it doesn't matter to me.' "No-one has ever made a record remotely like 'Upside Down', he claimed the following year.

Innovators aren't always understood, however. The Mary Chain have always been perfectionists in the studio, despite the studied spontaneity of their early records. Engineers usually have different artistic standards. Jim Reid: "The problem was that we spent more money and time on the idiots who run the studios. Like we would put the guitar in the corner and let it make noises, and the engineer would look at us as if we're mad. Then we spend two hours telling him that's what we want on our record, and he says, 'I've been doing this job for 25 years, and you can't do that, boys.' It's quite funny, really, we got into the studio and cracked open some beers and his eyes just popped out of his head."

Others were more enthusiastic. Stewart Cruickshank, producer of BBC Radio Scotland's *Rock On Scotland*, has championed many young Scottish bands on his show. He remembers: "This record came in that had just been released. I played it, and I couldn't believe it – I thought it was amazing! So the presenter Peter Easton played it on that night's show; we were the first people to play the single. The reaction in Scotland was quite remarkable; we had so many people asking about who the band were."

What The Jesus And Mary Chain had done was to combine the industrial sounds of Einsturzende Neubaten and Pere Ubu, the relentless churning backbeat of The Velvet Underground, and the pop melodies of early sixties California. Previous noise merchants in the avant-garde field had delighted in scaring away the customers. Casual elitism has always littered the avant-garde, and there is a perverse enthusiasm amongst its supporters for 'noise for noise's sake'. Like the 'art for art's sake' movement that swept the visual arts in the early years of this century, this credo was doomed to self-absorption, and abject failure. Without an audience, popular art has no reason to exist; and without being popular, art is useless. Anyone can impress a coterie of their friends; as the song says, that's what friends are for. The point, as Marx would have said if he had lived to be a rock critic, is to change the world.

Subversion has always been the name of The Mary Chain's game. But they are not prepared to skulk in the underground, and play at being dangerous artistic terrorists. They always wanted to be on *Top Of The Pops*, though on their own terms. 'Upside Down' didn't take them there; but it did top the independent charts. Having stalled at number two that Christmas behind The Toy Dolls' pseudo-punk 'Nellie The Elephant' (a fine example of what happens when revolt is turned into style), they reached number one in February, stayed there for three weeks; lost their position to The Smiths, and then regained it in March for another three weeks. By the spring of 1985, 'Upside Down' had sold around 35,000 copies, and it is now one of the biggest-selling indie singles of the eighties.

Student Demonstration Time

▶

CHAPTER 4

During November 1984, The Jesus And Mary Chain played at the Three Johns in Islington, where they were seen by the *NME*'s Neil Taylor. He casually referred to them in his review as "the best band in the world," though such pronouncements were commonplace in a music press which could only thrive by discovering the Next Big Thing. In the same month, the band sacked Murray Dalglish, and replaced him with another Creation signing – Bobby Gillespie of Primal Scream.

This was a move reminiscent of the formation of The Jefferson Airplane two decades earlier, when vocalist Marty Balin had approached guitarist Skip Spence with the offer of a role as the Airplane's drummer. In Primal Scream, Gillespie was a vocalist, not a percussionist, and his drumming abilities were slight. Jim Reid was suitably impressed, however: "When Bobby drums he only uses a floor tom and a snare. He can't play the fucking drums properly, but the way he plays them, standing up, creates such a good beat and is so visually attractive that it works." Musical virtuosity was scarcely the point, after all: "Our attitude has always been please your fucking self. We use loads of feedback to create noise; the whole idea of the sound is to create that spontaneous chaos and amplify it."

"Sometimes speed makes me feel like I could walk on water. Other times it makes me feel that if I tried to walk on water I'd sink without a trace. That's the only drug I participate in." (William Reid, September 1985.)

In December 1984, the group were busted for possession of amphetamine sulphate. On stage, Jim Reid wore a 'Heroin Thrills' T-shirt. He gleefully confessed to indulging in acid and speed. Were The Jesus And Mary Chain just another amphetamine rush in sound? Was their drug use a conscious attempt to echo the sixties psychedelia of Pink Floyd and The Velvets? Or was the entire image a pose, part of The Mary Chain's rebel construction along with the tight black leather and the affected shades?

Their cover of Pink Floyd's 'Vegetable Man' offered a clue. Syd Barrett's song, recorded as a demo shortly before he fell out of the group, was a straight blueprint for The Mary Chain's rendition; they simply turned up the volume and repeated the chorus, leaving the basic arrangement intact. Such devotion to 20-year-old models fitted uneasily alongside their public iconoclasm, and suggested that for all their boasts of breaking with tradition, The Mary Chain were very much aware of the sixties heritage. Their jagged sound represented a psychedelic nightmare, rather than the optimistic charging through barriers offered by the acid-rock bands of the sixties. Depression, not elation, was The Mary Chain's underlying theme. But they respected the past, instead of ignoring it, as the punk bands had pretended to do. And the drugs? They were used to cover up reality, not to explore it.

"Drugs can make you happy, but it's a sort of false happiness. My happiest moment ever was the first time I took speed. Sheer happiness It was totally phoney. It's no solution." (Jim Reid, July 1986.)

At the end of December, The Mary Chain appeared at London's ICA Rock Week, topping the bill over These Tender Virtues and Shelleyan Orphan. Bottles were thrown onstage during their performance, and there were press stories of a riot. Local councils, ever eager to win popular support by protecting their innocent voters from passing horsemen of the apocalypse, promptly banned The Mary Chain in several cities – a kneejerk reaction that doubled in tempo once *The Sun* had given the band their first national publicity, concentrating on violence and drugs.

As media attention increased, so the major record companies began to take an interest in 'The new Sex Pistols'. Jim Reid: "After the first single, we had a lot of interest from a few companies; we never approached them. The others said things like, 'You do this with us and we'll change your sound', so we went with WEA for a single deal." Even WEA were keen to sign the image rather than the substance: "The longterm deals they were asking of us were a joke. Like no feedback on records, or put a little bit of feedback on, just to please the fans. It seems that 'do what we tell you and you'll make lots of money' is the deal. But the one-off deal gives us the power to do what we want. For the moment, it seems we're this month's scruffs!"

New readers begin here. The Sex Pistols were signed to EMI after press reports of violence at their gigs. A few weeks later, their behaviour so outraged the company's executives that the band were given £25,000 to leave the label. They then signed with A&M, where the pattern was repeated – this time after a week in which several of the company's leading artists had threatened to desert A&M if The Pistols were signed to the label. The Pistols thrived on publicity – on the tales of vomiting at airports, assaulting record company staff, and trashing plush executives' offices. Manager Malcolm McLaren sat back and counted the money, while the group lapped up the publicity and wondered why they weren't being allowed to play live. Now read on.

The Mary Chain signed with WEA in January 1985, visiting the company's Broadwick Street offices to clinch the deal. Here hyperbole and hype join hands. Did the band really steal money from WEA MD Rob Dickens' jacket? No. Did they really destroy his office? No. Did they harass staff members and threaten them with violence? Of course not. But the stories appeared in the press, and manager Alan McGee did nothing to deny them. In fact . . .

"At WEA they expect you to come in wearing a suit, or at least to act and behave the way they do. They all speak in clichés like, 'That's cool for me, is it cool for you?' Maybe we did knock over a few things, but it was an accident!"
(Jim Reid, February 1985.)

"We're meant to have wrecked a record company office, but all we did was write on a few posters. It all started when part of a ZZ Top display fell down."
(William Reid, March 1985.)

"We're still not allowed in there."
(Jim Reid, March 1985.)

In March, The Jesus And Mary Chain journeyed to Belgium for a television appearance to promote their second single. According to manager McGee, the band destroyed the specially-built set laid on for them; damaged the expensive audio equipment on the set; and then deigned to be interviewed on a couch, while drummer Bobby Gillespie and an unnamed girl "were practically having sex, and everyone was trying to ignore it."

It transpired that the TV producer had asked them to destroy the set as part of their act; that one microphone stand suffered minor cuts and bruises; and that Gillespie – well, let the producer explain: "Having sex? I don't think so. He was only kissing her. If he thinks that's having sex, then he has more problems than I thought."

Back in London, The Mary Chain headlined their biggest gig so far, at the North London Polytechnic. The venue overbooked the hall, leaving hundreds of frustrated fans locked outside; the police were summoned when Gillespie and Hart attempted to smash the locks. Support band Meat Whiplash took the stage, and vocalist Paul McDermott threw an empty wine bottle into the audience. He was then attacked by four members of the crowd, and the band's set was abandoned. Fellow Creation-ists The Jasmine Minks survived their set intact, but trouble flared again when The Mary Chain kept the audience waiting for an hour before appearing onstage.

After less than 20 minutes, however, the band left the stage, and the tension turned to riot. The audience began throwing cans at where the band were hiding behind the stage curtains, before mounting the stage to trash their PA and equipment. Police soon became involved in the fracas, and fighting continued for some time before order was restored.

After the gig, North London Poly representatives commented: "The Jesus And Mary Chain went on ridiculously late, kept the audience waiting and then had two equipment breakdowns. That's what caused the trouble."

The Mary Chain, through Alan McGee, issued a statement of their own. "The Jesus And Mary Chain deny all responsibility for the proceedings on Friday night," it began. "Friday night proved that people are crying out for the first division excitement that The Jesus And Mary Chain provides. In an abstract way, the audience were not smashing up the hall, they were smashing up pop music. The Jesus And Mary Chain are putting excitement back into rock 'n' roll, and promoters will have to bear the consequences. This is truly art as terrorism."

The stupidity of this statement speaks for itself. It belongs firmly in the tradition of anarchist bullshit, the belief that destruction is a creative act and can be turned into an end in itself. At the time, McGee's statement alienated many of the band's potential supporters. Those who were excited by their musical adventurism were repelled by the juvenile crassness of their publicity machine.

The band slowly came to realise this themselves. In May 1985, Jim Reid was still scattering the blame elsewhere: "It wasn't our making. The students were to blame for keeping ticket holders outside all night. They could nae run a minodge." Six months later, William commented: "Five people were fighting down the front, and the guy from the NME called it a riot. He must have been taking acid at the time. I think people then started to come to our gigs and expect a riot. I hate it, I despise it. It gets in the way in terms of getting more gigs, and it gets in the way of our image. We're trying to present ourselves as a serious group, not a Cockney Rejects Oi Oi type of group." Maybe William should have issued his own press statement, instead of allowing the "art as terrorism" line to emerge.

The North London Poly affair had two effects: it distracted attention from the band's music, and it devastated their roster of gigs. Throughout the rest of 1985, the band were unable to string together more than three British gigs in a row, without promoters and councils calling a halt.

In September, the band played another London show, at the Electric Ballroom in Camden. And once again, the gig degenerated into violence. After the usual hour's delay while the band's minimal stage equipment was set up, The Mary Chain played their customary sub-20-minute set. An occasional bottle was thrown at the band while they were onstage, but afterwards a small section of the audience smashed up the amplification equipment. Lights were smashed, and several people were cut by flying glass. This time, Alan McGee refused to comment.

Although the band's violent image and provocative press statements undoubtedly helped to attract trouble to their gigs, there was a certain amount of self-fulfilment to their problems. The band insisted on playing for 20 minutes and no longer; and although anyone who had read press coverage of the band should have been aware of this fact, they were likely to lose their cool when the 20 minutes had expired and they were still in a pre-orgasmic state.

No-one would have batted an eyelid at a 20-minute set in the sixties, of course, when anything longer was a luxury that only superstars enjoyed. The package tours that represented the most common form of pop performance before 1967 regularly featured eight or 10 acts – and only the headliner would be able to perform more than four or five songs. The Beatles, for example, never played longer than 32 minutes at any one of their concerts between 1963 and 1966.

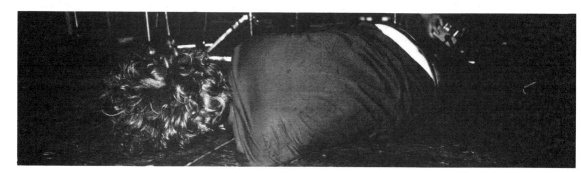

By the late sixties, the average guitar solo lasted longer than 32 minutes, and so live performances were extended to hold the new sound. Headliners regularly played for two hours or so, getting through 10 or maybe 12 songs with lengthy solos (one of them being the obligatory 20-minute drum solo). The Grateful Dead took this trend to its ultimate, sometimes gigging for six or seven hours when under the spell of some particularly fine acid.

The dynamism of the punk bands, who lost more sweat in a song than the Dead did in a week, shortened stage acts once more. J&MC heroes The Ramones represented the pinnacle of the new ethos, stripping their songs down to 90 seconds or less, and on a slick night turning out 20 near identical songs in a little over the half-hour – separated only by a New York-accented count-in.

The Mary Chain followed this tradition. "We play 25 minutes maximum because there's never been a group good enough to play any longer," explained Jim Reid in May 1985. "Never has been, never will be. People get bored, the groups get boring. Anyway, we've only got enough songs to play for that long. Ten songs, none of them longer than two-and-a-half minutes." On other occasions, he was even more dismissive: "If we only play 20 minutes that's an indication that we're bored out of our skulls. In any case, 20 minutes of us is worth any amount of money." Tell it to the North London Poly, Jim.

THE HISTORY
of **FEEDBACK**
PART ②

Every sixties club band playing deafening R&B in a crowded, low-ceilinged club was familiar with feedback, which was an inevitable accompaniment to their performance. It took imagination to realise that the uncontrollable sound had its creative uses – that the accidental howl of electric circuits overloading could be channelled into purposeful noise. In the mid-sixties, London R&B clubs resounded to the howl of feedback, as guitarists like Eric Clapton, Pete Townshend, Jeff Beck and Brian Jones drove their amplifiers into overdrive.

On record, though, the power of these bands was emasculated by recording engineers groomed on trad jazz, string quartets and MOR ballads. The engineer was there to prevent distortion, not to capture it; and it took the pioneering genius of American producer Shel Talmy to allow the grungy, unsettling live sound of the electric guitar to be captured on tape. With The Kinks, he encouraged Dave Davies to play at concert volume, with a knitting needle driven deep into the heart of his amp to produce a gritty, disturbing sound. Records like 'You Really Got Me' and 'All Day And All Of The Night' were unrestrained romps across the bare minimum of chord changes, which drew feedback howls of protest from musical purists.

But it was Pete Townshend of The Who who turned feedback into art – Pop-Art, to be precise. Their début, 'I Can't Explain', was relatively restrained. 'Anyway, Anyhow, Anywhere', issued early in 1965, was something else entirely. Townshend took a long solo, channelling his feedback into throbbing chords, dive bomber runs across the speakers, occasional ghostly shrieks – all perfectly controlled, but hinting at total mayhem, while Keith Moon's drums and Nicky Hopkins' piano rumbled underneath. Television's *Ready Steady Go* abandoned miming and went live just in time for The Who to repeat the process in millions of British homes. Townshend's white noise powered from the speakers, while the cameramen flicked from musician to musician in a desperate attempt to match the fire of the sound.

Pete Townshend

In live performance, Townshend took noise to its ultimate, turning the amplifiers to maximum before crashing his guitar against them, dividing the body from the neck, and pummelling the unfortunate instrument into the ground for the benefit of any national press photographers who happened to be passing. He was expressing the frustration of the mods, of course, smashed, blocked and repressed by the soft options and fussy morals of contemporary Britain. He was also creating an unholy, blasphemous racket.

Jeff Beck of The Yardbirds took up the feedback challenge. He had replaced Eric 'Slowhand' Clapton, a blues purist who frowned upon the destruction of sacred instruments and the transition from emotion into aggression. Beck was equally devoted to his craft, but although he shared few of Townshend's social theories and personal hang-ups, he was fascinated by the theoretical possibilities of the guitar. Later he matured into jazz-rock fusion, the replacement of feeling with technique; but first he allowed himself a few months' relaxation with feedback.

On 'Yardbirds', the group's only British studio album, Beck showed off his total versatility – rifling off blues riffs, delicate arpeggios, stinging runs and atonal barrages at will. The 'Nazz Is Blue' stole a Freddie King riff, and added a banshee wail of feedback; and 'Lost Woman' had a guitar/harmonica battle that Beck ended with a high-pitched, over-amplified whine from his guitar. Everything was controlled, to prove that Beck was an artist, not a showman or an emotional wildman; and once he had demonstrated the technique, Beck moved on.

One guitarist outmanoeuvred all his English rivals, Beck, Clapton and Townshend – Jimi Hendrix. His music knew no boundaries, which is why he is claimed by a score of competing traditions as their mentor. He could play jazz, blues, rock and white noise with equal skill; more remarkably, he could combine them all into one devastating attack on musical categorisation.

Like most musical innovators, Hendrix spawned many bastard sons. You can blame him for jazz-rock, heavy metal, techno-flash – and the ear-splitting roar of The Jesus And Mary Chain. For Hendrix realised, as no other musician had, the potential of feedback for painting pictures in the ether. Playing at immense volume, to the point where it was difficult to distinguish his chording from his feedback, he conjured up a swirling, encompassing fog of noise, that (with the aid of psychedelic drugs) you could mould into the heaven or hell of your choice. From orgy to apocalypse is a short road, and Hendrix combined the two with ease. Using a battery of pedals and effects – wah-wah, sustain, fuzz – he transformed music into sound and sound into vision. And he did it all with humour and lyricism, revealing an air of gentleness behind the overpowering assault of his music. The sea of possibilities he opened is still uncharted.

Few musicians could play like Beck, still fewer like Hendrix. For them, noise was a vehicle, rather than an end – part of the journey, rather than the destination. It took four art-crazed New Yorkers to turn the creation of feedback from a musical choice into a moral one.

Jimi Hendrix

Wake The World

▶

CHAPTER 5

In February 1985, The Jesus And Mary Chain issued their second single – and their first on WEA's subsidiary label, Blanco y Negro. WEA originally refused to press the B-side, 'Suck', but relented when given the alternative, a song called 'Jesus Fuck'. 'Never Understand' was the A-side, which gave The Mary Chain their first national hit at the end of March.

"Call us 1980s British Beach Boys or whatever. But everything we make sounds like a pop song, even if it's different to any other pop song and even if it might not suit the daytime radio programmers. I think 'Never Understand' is fairly conventional."
(Jim Reid, March 1985.)

"It's too much of a racket for the DJs. People will tune in and think, 'What's that whistling noise?'"
(Douglas Hart, March 1985.)

'Never Understand' made few concessions to WEA's major label status. It opened with the dentist's drill whine of William Reid's guitar, followed by Douglas Hart's tentative bass. The song was classic three-chord pop, a surf refugee from the early sixties transported into the centre of a hurricane. While Jim Reid relived the innocent sound of West Coast fun fun fun, William layered feedback and distortion on to the track, adding a fresh hammer from hell after every verse and chorus. For the climax, Jim uttered primal screams while the guitars roared across the speakers with an apocalyptic fury. 'Upside Down' seemed slight by comparison.

The white noise was a mental backdrop to the song; as the feedback grew larger, so the ears strained more desperately to hear the lyrics, to retain the melody at the heart of the mayhem. The simplicity of the song structure only doubled the power: the Reids had taken a naïve, joyous form and perverted it to their own ends. The rumbling bass riffs and steady rhythms of the classic surf records were retained, but the vocal harmonies were replaced by stunning waves of sound. The 1960s Beach Boys celebrated California in their music, and lived out its darkest excesses in their lives. The 1980s British Beach Boys combined both extremes in a wash of shadows and light.

The flipside revealed a new angle on The Mary Chain's music. 'Suck' was a crazed and confused marriage between Public Image Ltd. and Joy Division, all pulsing bass and deadening rhythms – while on the 12" single (a marketing ploy the Mary

Chain couldn't escape) was a cover version of Vic Godard's 'Ambition'. The Subway Sect's original updated the whimsical pop of late sixties Syd Barrett, with a tinny organ and toy drum sound. The Mary Chain performed the song straight, and then buried it beneath a muffling feedback wall that removed all the original version's delicate optimism. They were occasionally accused of psychedelia, but they denied it vehemently; their treatment of psychedelic excess in their music suggested that they were protesting too much.

'Jesus Fuck' became the band's prime concern in April and May. The track was grungy, weighed down by the band's impersonation of The Stooges, but the fact that WEA had rejected the song made them all the more keen to release it. Alan McGee first announced a 12″ reissue of 'Upside Down' that would include the song; test pressings were made, but the single never appeared. Then the band realised that they could achieve more publicity by demanding that WEA issue the track as the flipside of their next single. By now, the title had changed to 'Jesus Suck', but the pressing plants still refused to touch it. The single was delayed, and The Mary Chain issued another of their self-dramatising 'statements': "This is completely typical of the stale-minded music business. The Jesus And Mary Chain continually try to break the music business stereotype, but on this occasion the cliché has affected even us. The group is disgusted by it all." Possibly aware that their reaction was as much a cliché as Warner Brothers', the band desisted from issuing further Clash-like communiqués in this manner.

The combination of the band's name, and the title of this banned song, helped to ensure suitably critical national press coverage throughout the spring. A year later, Jim Reid looked back on the farrago with a jaundiced eye: " 'Jesus Suck' was just downright repulsion at how sacred the name Jesus was. It was actually called 'Jesus Fuck', but we were told we couldn't release it called that, so we called it 'Jesus Suck' and they didn't release it anyway. Jesus Christ has been followed and preached about for 2,000 years, and people seriously think that this little group making a fairly obscure little record called 'Jesus Fuck' is going to do anybody any harm whatsoever? It's kind of ridiculous. I'd still like that record to come out, but the truth of the matter is it's not very good."

Late in May, 'You Trip Me Up' reached the shops, with no mention of Jesus beyond the group's name. It was their loudest, most extreme record yet – but with the simplest, loveliest melody. Stripped of the terrifying feedback adornments that gave it such crushing power, 'You Trip Me Up' would have been ideal raw material for Phil Spector's Wall Of Sound. The Reids used similar techniques to Spector, crushing layer upon layer of noise into a tight, explosive ball. The emotional effect was also comparable. Spector's most titanic productions juxtaposed mighty orchestras and single-tracked, emotive vocals. The Mary Chain updated the cacophony, and left the vocals cool and detached. The tension was in the gap between the agony of the accompaniment, and the neurotic alienation of the voices.

"Nobody has made a record like 'You Trip Me Up'," commented Jim Reid the following year. "Maybe someone's used those chords before, but I couldn't give a damn about the chords. That was a completely warped and twisted record, and it almost got in the Top 40. To me, that is quite subversive, a danger to the established music business."

The gap between live and studio sound is rarely remarked upon, although anyone who has attended a live rock concert will be aware that the textured separation of vinyl bears little relation to the distorted and often deafening impact of stage performances. 'Just Out Of Reach', the flipside of the 7″ edition of 'You Trip Me Up', came close to marrying the two presentations. The feedback guitar sound on this track is pure treble, crackling in the ears like an over-amplified live gig, only without the pain. The noise is disturbing, as it pricks parts of the brain that are usually soothed by music, not provoked. The song was incidental; what counted was the noise, and the sense of unease it aroused.

'Boyfriend's Dead' completed the 12″ package. The guitar riffing conjured up unhappy memories of the satanic rock of Black Sabbath, while the frenzied, tormented vocals were once again inspired by the extravagances of John Lydon's Public Image. Like 'Suck', it contained worrying hints that The Mary Chain might descend into a doomy, joyless sub-Joy Division mood, losing the tension of feedback and melody that was their strongest key.

Despite their best endeavours, 'You Trip Me Up' sold no better than 'Never Understand', and The Jesus And Mary Chain were still a long way from competing with Wham! for a place on *Top Of The Pops*. Both singles had made the bottom end of the Top 50 quite easily, but without daytime radio airplay their potential audience was limited.

John Peel, whose Radio One show has been a beacon for the British underground since the late sixties, had been a consistent supporter of The Mary Chain. He gave them a session on his late night show around the time that 'Upside Down' was released; 'Taste The Floor', 'Never Understand', 'In A Hole' and 'You Trip Me Up' were débuted there. He also plugged the single consistently; and offered the group a second session in February 1985, where they performed three more as yet unrecorded songs, 'Just Like Honey', 'Inside Me' and 'The Living End'. He had followed through by giving 'Never Understand' and 'You Trip Me Up' regular exposure.

The Mary Chain had also appeared on the newly-shortened *Whistle Test* in March 1985, performing another new song, the cacophonous 'In A Hole'. The month before, they had played in Liverpool, a gig attended by the production team of Channel 4's *The Tube*, a pop show that shared the aims of The Mary Chain – excitement, commercial appeal, and an alternative approach. "They despised us *totally*," said Jim Reid gleefully after the event. "We'd been told to be on our best behaviour, so we got hideously drunk and played totally haywire."

Tube producer Ken Scorfield claimed that he rejected the band when he saw the audience leaving in droves during the gig. "It was a shambles," he said defensively.

The Mary Chain were still convinced that they were commercial; and stardom was their avowed aim. "Our ambition is to be superstars," Jim confirmed in March 1985, "Superstars doing what we are now. I'd like to have that kind of power. We're not interested in cult status, hiding in a cupboard and making records for 20 people."

"Superstars doing what we are now" – there was the rub. As WEA and the other major labels had realised after the release of 'Upside Down', The Mary Chain's anarchic rebelliousness was extremely marketable; the revolution would not only be televised, but the merchandising rights would be sold to Coca-Cola. But the sound – that harsh, asexual, unromantic noise – was not the stuff of which romantic media images were made. Hence WEA's attempts to persuade J&MC to forgo the feedback, or just insert a couple of bars of noise as a trademark, a taste of rebellion which the mass media could swallow.

The band were attempting to reunite two decades of division in the music business. In the fifties and early sixties, music was defined by its commercial appeal. Singles either sold or they didn't; lack of sales equalled failure. Outside the London clubs, there was no such concept as cult appeal; that was a retrospective gesture of support for bands like The Creation, The Action and The Artwoods, who refused to sacrifice their artistic credentials for commercial ends, and paid the price by being ignored by the media. Pop wasn't art, but commerce: a division that made success and failure easy to define.

The Beatles changed that, as they did so much else in the
music business. And, as usual, the benefits were mixed. Their
'Sergeant Pepper' album in 1967 received lavish attention not
just from pop writers, but also from classical music critics, who
were delighted to find popular music that apparently had a
serious intent. Pop was now art, not just entertainment; and so
music quickly divided into the overground, commercial pop of
the singles chart, aimed blatantly at teens and sub-teens; and the
underground rock music of the albums chart.

For a while, the major artists – The Beatles, The Stones, The
Who – crossed over into both camps, scoring hit singles and
prestigious album sales. But by the end of the sixties, hit singles
equalled 'selling out', and the dividing line between pop and
rock grew ever wider.

The appeal of glam rock in the early seventies was that it gave
a new generation of teenagers a music of their own, that didn't
require study or appreciation, merely enjoyment. At the same
time, the androgynous image of artists like David Bowie, The
Sweet and Marc Bolan gave glam an air of danger missing from
the concoctions that had dominated the singles chart since the
late sixties.

Glam died as its audience grew older, and demanded more sophistication; more meaning behind the make-up. Pop wobbled pathetically between middle-aged entertainment and childish confectionery, until punk briefly reunited teenagers and students, kids and critics. For around six months, the plight of The Sex Pistols bonded a generation: harassed for their appearance, despised for their music, banned for their violence. Thereafter, as The Pistols plunged from rock icons to greedy professionals, and The Clash fell for their own rebel rhetoric, new wave sprang up and the chasm widened again. By the early eighties, rock stood polarised between the contrived glamour of Duran Duran, and the grey security of an indie scene still dominated by dear departed Joy Division.

By 1985, the indie labels had lost their major talents, their sales, and their purpose. Like the avant-garde, they revelled in their lack of popularity, taking lack of commercial acceptance as proof of their success. In real terms, they were irrelevant, gaining no converts, making no artistic progress. The Jesus And Mary Chain offered a way out, a path away from self-absorption and back towards the real world.

The Mary Chain were all too aware of the pitfalls of the indie scene. Jim Reid: "If we played the game by the rules, we'd be on an independent now and go on and on for seven or eight years playing the same music." (Could he possibly be referring to those arch indie heroes, The Fall?) "If people really hate majors so much, they'd realise what we're doing is more of a threat to majors than anything you can do on an indie. I'm not dead set against indies; they're a stepping stone, they give people a chance. We're part of WEA now, OK, but before we were part of it WEA was 100 per cent shit. Now it's a little bit good."
"As long as there is a Top 40," he confirmed later in 1985, "I wanna be there, because that's where we do most good. We don't do any good selling 2,000 indie singles."

That Same Song

▶

CHAPTER 6

After the demise of the Postcard label in 1982, and the inability of Orange Juice, Aztec Camera, Josef K or their offshoots to make a telling creative advance on their early singles, Scottish music was left in a kind of limbo. As in London, some musicians responded by returning to Glasgow's favourite music, soul – dressing up black American rhythms in party costumes. Others ploughed the same barren furrows as the London and Manchester indie bands, choosing a ghetto of their own making.

The arrival of The Jesus And Mary Chain represented an escape route. In attitude and sound, they were a welcome relief from the shuffling beat of the indie scene or the soul-less lounge lizard meanderings of the night-club denizens. It's simplistic to describe The Mary Chain as a political band; they have been consistently dismissive of the Red Wedge brigade, who believe that a trendy T-shirt and a right-on lyric sheet can change the world. But in a country that felt itself to be under foreign domination, governed by a party which it had rejected decisively at the polls, and used as a testing-ground for any policies too controversial to be tried on the English, any breath of revolt brought fresh air. The Mary Chain's sound encompassed anger, dissent and self-belief – all qualities that Scotland had once possessed, and now needed to rekindle.

There was no sudden rush to the barricades, or march of Mary Chain fans on Downing Street. But the band did inspire a revitalisation of the Scottish underground. The fanzine scene, dead since the folding of Postcard, re-emerged with new strength, covering not just The Mary Chain and the other Creation-ists, but a wave of new Scottish talent that was equally loud and uncompromising. BBC Scotland's *Rock On Scotland* show, long a bastion of the best homegrown music, was suddenly inundated with tapes from new outfits. Many just copied The Mary Chain wholesale, from feedback to song titles; others took the example, and built their own assembly of melody and dissonance. Groups like The BMX Bandits and The Soup Dragons, for example, came through after The Mary Chain, and although they were by no means copyists, the influence was clear.

Creation Records, though based in London, was open to Scottish talent still; and one signing which had particular links to The Mary Chain was Meat Whiplash. The band had opened The Jesus And Mary Chain's infamous gig at the North London Polytechnic, and spurred the audience into frenzies of violence by their careless discarding of empty wine bottles. True to form, Alan McGee recognised a new hype in the making, and he instantly signed Meat Whiplash to his label.

Like The Mary Chain, Meat Whiplash claimed to be teenagers; this time it was true. The band took their name from a song by The Fire Engines, a Scottish band who had emerged alongside the Postcard troupe, and whose tight, swirling rhythms introduced traces of Captain Beefheart into the prevailing atmosphere of psychedelia. That was as far as the influence went, however: on record, and they only made one, Meat Whiplash were pure Jesus And Mary Chain.

It made sense, then, for McGee to persuade the J&MC to produce Meat Whiplash's Creation single. It received ecstatic reviews, leading Neil Taylor in the *NME* to pronounce that it was one of the greatest records of all time. And in a strange way, he was right.

'Don't Slip Up' followed The Mary Chain blueprint exactly – horrific feedback, three-chord melody, repetitive lyrics, solid backbeat. They brought to the song an additional ingredient that was beyond The Mary Chain: incompetence. William Reid (a genius, in his brother's estimation) had refined his use of feedback to perfection, allowing him a remarkable range of sonic effects in the studio. Whiplash only had two positions on their amps: 'off' and 'loud'. 'Don't Slip Up' sounded like the end of the world, and it guaranteed headaches to anyone unprepared for the fury of its assault. Midway through, the band threw in a classic early sixties trick, lifted straight from a Beach Boys' record like 'Dance Dance Dance'. The guitars screeched to a halt, while the bass and drums played a simple two-bar break that both relieved and doubled the tension. The ending was chaotic, with the band unable to stop at the same time; but the damage had been done.

"I think they were impressed by how bad we were," commented drummer Michael Kerr of their illustrious producers. This judgement was confirmed by the B-side, the horrendous 'Here It Comes' – a pedestrian dirge which showed no indication of coming to terms with the band's potential.

"It'd be a mistake to think there's some big scene going on in East Kilbride, because there isn't one," Michael Kerr explained when the single was released. "The place is totally dead, it's like the Milton Keynes of Scotland. It's just a coincidence that us and The Mary Chain come from the same area." Well, maybe. Certainly without the home town link, it is difficult to imagine that The Mary Chain would have become involved with a band who aped their own style so blatantly. Meat Whiplash were the classic one-hit-wonder: they cut one brilliant song, briefly made the indie charts, and then split up in May 1986 without issuing another record.

Before their split, however, they shared one memorable night with The Jesus And Mary Chain. In the autumn of 1985, The Mary Chain returned to Glasgow, to headline at the Splash One! club at 46 West George Street. Splash One! had been one of the few venues willing to allow The Mary Chain to play over the previous year, and they had also allowed Meat Whiplash several gigs.

Whiplash opened the show with a stunning display of incompetence. Their first song had to be abandoned when they were unable to play together in time; and their blitzkrieg set comprised wild feedback and much flailing of microphones. Audience response was, to say the least, lukewarm.

Elsewhere in Britain, The Jesus And Mary Chain had been attracting riotous behaviour from their supporters. The Glasgow promoters had read their press coverage carefully, and took no chances. The show was only advertised on the BBC's *Rock On Scotland*, in the hope of dissuading random hooligan elements from attending. A lavish display of bouncers was booked for the night, and body-searches were carried out on the door. Then, when it was time for The Mary Chain to play, a row of 15 bouncers stood across the front of the stage, to make sure that the stars could not be injured by their audience. The Mary Chain, meanwhile, waltzed unconcernedly through the audience towards the stage without a finger being lain on them. They played their usual 20-minute set from behind the protective wall, bellowed out a final blast of feedback, and then walked back off the stage, between the bouncers and back among the audience in perfect safety.

THE HISTORY *of* FEEDBACK PART ③

If you received royalties every time your name was dropped, The Velvet Underground would be millionaires. Lou Reed, John Cale, Mo Tucker and Sterling Morrison enjoyed their brief moment of commercial success when their début album, 'The Velvet Underground And Nico', reached number 182 in the Billboard charts. Cale left to work as a producer after their second LP, 'White Light/White Heat'. Reed carried The Velvets through two subsequent albums, finally jettisoning his band during the mixing of 'Loaded' in 1970, and beginning a career as a soloist, chronicler of low life, and imitation heroin addict.

By the early seventies, David Bowie had recorded his Velvets tribute, 'Queen Bitch', and the band had begun to claim some posthumous glory. Retrospectives of their less-than-glittering career littered the British rock press, and a fresh generation of teenage rebels discovered that mid-seventies pomp-rock wasn't their only option. Alongside The Stooges and The New York Dolls, The Velvet Underground were the prime inspiration for the British punk and new wave movements, and subsequently it has been *de rigeur* to claim their influence if you want to enjoy any artistic credibility in Britain.

The sheer range of The Velvets' sonic experiments has enabled lazy rock journalists to brand any number of stylists as Velvets imitators. It's like comparing a band to The Beatles without specifying whether you mean 'She Loves You' or 'Strawberry

Fields Forever'. Anyone who ignores The Velvets' sound, though, is condemned to fall short of it; and scores more have chosen to repeat it, or else perish in the attempt.

"I know it sounds like a complete cliché to say, but I've always been a big Velvet Underground fan, and the effect I want to have on people is the effect that it has on me looking at pictures of Lou Reed, John Cale and Sterling Morrison in 1966. The photographs of them in Andy Warhol's Factory contain just about everything that made their music so awesome. That's what we're trying to do – our words, our music, our photographs. It should all be that one thing."
(Jim Reid, November 1985.)

Those photos – with black leather, shades, a cool disdain for the camera – reveal where the Reids borrowed much of their visual image. But they didn't need The Velvets for that – they could have found similar icons in James Dean, Marlon Brando, The Rolling Stones or The Clash. The Velvets' biggest contribution to The Mary Chain, and to rock music as a whole, was their use of noise. In the hands of The Velvets, noise has never washed so white.

Once again, it was the contrasts that made the impact. Lou Reed cut his teeth on late fifties pop, the sub-doowop vocal stylings of New York groups black and white, epitomised by supercool Dion and his Belmonts. Then in the early sixties, as wave after wave of new pop soared over the horizon from California to Liverpool, Reed found himself in the Pickwick Records factory for imitating hits. Pickwick's enterprise was an ironic satire on the legendary Brill Building, the songwriting capital of the early sixties. Instead of inventing classic songs, they copied them – rushing albums of ersatz surf music or Merseybeat into the stores, hoping to catch every passing wave with an earnings potential.

John Cale, Velvet Underground

Lou Reed found himself recording dance tunes, motorcycle songs, sub-Mersey rockers, phoney R&B; and being Lou Reed, he used the same three garage-rock chords every time. His earliest compositions, like 'Do The Orchid' and 'Little Cycle Annie', are crazed perversions of teenage American music, close enough to the real thing to confuse the middle-aged Pickwick executives, but not their kids.

Still, Reed had found his niche. Add John Cale, schooled in the avant-garde music of LaMonte Young; and the sordid cultural milieu that the duo found in the denizens of Pop-Artist Andy Warhol; and the seeds of The Velvet Underground were planted.

Their first album is still an utterly staggering record, totally of its period and place and yet unanachronistic two decades later. It chronicles a world of savagery, sex, drugs and despair, all disturbingly recounted without emotion. Characters live, suffer and die, and no-one cares as long as there are fresh thrills in the morning. It is an aura that – as Jean Stein's book *Edie* chronicles – the inhabitants of the Factory carried over into real life; and it has appealed to the alienated and the thrill-seeking ever since.

Lou Reed's genius was double-edged. In his lyrics, he constructed imagery so tight that the songs retain all their power when played on acoustic guitar. To that extent, the noise of The Velvets was unnecessary: the evil was already in the words. The music was merely the soundtrack to the ultimate *film noir*, an aural account of hell. But the music entered another dimension when Reed's howling guitar was joined by the spectral scream of John Cale's electric viola. 'Black Angel's Death Song', 'European Son' and 'Heroin' were unlike anything in previous rock history – they had a demonic, unyielding power that distorted the capacity to think. And all the time, the musicians were standing calmly in front of their squealing amplifiers, like ghostly harbingers of Shakespearian doom.

Iggy Pop

'White Light/White Heat' was equally devastating. Recorded in ill-funded sessions at the cheapest studios available, it was a producer's nightmare – possibly the worst recorded album ever made by a name band. But the lack of hi-fidelity took nothing away from the raw drive of the music. The 17 minutes of 'Sister Ray', a one-chord paean to (if rumours are to be believed) The Kinks' Ray Davies, was the album's cornerstone – a grinding amalgam of decadence and booming feedback, topped with Reed's sly sado-masochistic lyrics.

But it was 'I Heard Her Call My Name' that was the clearest hint to the future. Lou Reed took the modal guitar virtuosity of The Byrds' 'Eight Miles High' to its logical extremes, flailing notes and chords into a chaotic blitz of sound. 'I felt my mind split open,' he sang, before guiding his guitar into the midst of the brain with a surgeon's skill and delight. This was as far as Reed could go – for a decade, at least. Future Velvets records retreated towards acoustic instruments and a quiet air of gloom, rather than the full-bore apocalypse of 'White Light/ White Heat'. But the example was there for anyone to follow.

"After us, the perfect record is 'I Wanna Be Your Dog' by The Stooges, but the horrible guitar solo fucks it up. 'Heroin' by The Velvet Underground is almost perfect, but I don't like the violin."
(William Reid, November 1985.)

The Stooges – led by James Osterburg/Iggy Pop – combined The Velvets' disrespect for the ear with the three-chord grunge of the garage bands. Iggy screamed and purred, and cut into his flesh with broken glass; while behind him The Stooges powered their way into the only chords they knew. Over two albums, 'The Stooges' and 'Funhouse', they created the ultimate garage nightmare – a David Cronenburg movie in music. No subtleties here – the massacre was the message.

Diamond Head
▶
CHAPTER 7

"It never occurred to me then, but I realise now that the songs never came across when we started playing. We knew what the songs were like; we'd written them and played them on acoustic guitars, and we thought they were wonderful. Then we'd play at The Living Room or something and it never occurred to us that people couldn't actually hear the songs. I'd be doing 'Upside Down' and I'd think it was like a bird singing in the trees or something. But the crowd would just be hearing this awful noise, they wouldn't get the song and I'd be amazed. After the gigs, people would say, 'Oh, it's all very well, but you're gonna have to write a song one of these days.' We thought they had cloth ears or something."
(Jim Reid, August 1986.)

The Jesus And Mary Chain shambled into the public eye as anarchistic rebels, proto-punks bent on immolating the music industry. Once they abandoned Alan McGee's manifesto-like statements, however, and spoke up for themselves, they began to sound more like tortured singer-songwriters, refugees from the era when James Taylor was greeted by *Melody Maker* as Rock's Messiah – the first of the second comings.

The band's maelstrom of noise, bathed in shallow lighting and fuelled by their neo-violent stance, effectively masked not only the content of their songs, but also their structure. On record, the quaintly old-fashioned construction of their material was dimly decipherable beneath the feedback. In concert, there was just the noise, and the songs were only vehicles for a fresh blast of amplification.

By the summer of 1985, having produced what they considered to be three classic singles, The Mary Chain were anxious to prove their credentials as songwriters as well as revolutionaries. In their defence, they had never made any secret of their abilities: as early as December 1984, Jim Reid had proclaimed: "We've got good songs . . . certain people just won't realise that. You could play our songs on an acoustic guitar, they'd still be good."

As promoters and local councils quailed before the threat of a second North London Poly experience, The Mary Chain began to toy with the idea of doing just that. "Ah, The Jesus And Mary Chain – a feedback group," remarked Jim Reid in November 1985, mouthing the popular conception of the band. "It was becoming a travelling circus. That's why we've decided to do some acoustic gigs, because everybody expects us to arrive on stage drunk and make a hell of a racket. We just don't like the idea of somebody else deciding what we are. We can do anything."

Acoustic gigs would certainly separate the serious men from the toy boys. Faced by an acoustic guitar, a microphone and an audience seething with beer and whiskey, more experienced musicians than the Reids had lost their nerve. Ironically, one of the few eighties bandleaders to risk the acoustic route and survive had been Roddy Frame, leader of Scotland's Aztec Camera – and the arch example, to the Reids, of all that was most contemptible in the Postcard scene.

As it transpired, the pudding never had to be eaten. William and Jim Reid planned to play unannounced acoustic sets as a support act to American hardcore band Sonic Youth in the autumn of 1985; but when the news leaked out, and the prospect arose of more J&MC live hysteria, the Reids pulled out.

"The feedback could go out next week. It'll only last as long as we want it to. We're not going to make the same kind of records for 20 years. We all love acoustic records, and one day we're going to make acoustic records."
(Jim Reid, March 1985.)

Jim: "The actual fact that we use guitars is actually quite unimportant. We just happen to be familiar with them, just because they're the obvious things to use when you start making music. If we could get that same noise out of an oboe, we would do. If we could get it out of a clarinet, we would. Our music is probably more classical than anything else. If we'd been around in 1966, we might have been a trash group, but nowadays the whole idea is totally outdated."

William: "Trash is like a cheap and nasty sound. Ours is about as classy as you can get. Ours is actually a very carefully crafted sound."
(November 1985.)

Two Jesus And Mary Chain singles were released in October 1985 – one official, the other totally unauthorised. Together, they represented the two sides of the group, the monster and the musician. The 'Riot' single actually included no J&MC music, although its aural impact was very similar to the band's early 45s. As its name suggested, it was an *audio-verité* record of the North London Poly gig, beginning as the band left the stage and members of the audience took their place.

The record, issued in a limited run of 100 copies by the Swansea label Fierce Records, was an incoherent mix of random conversation and violence, with amplifiers crashing and bottles flying. With sly humour, it was packaged alongside J&MC memorabilia – pieces of Bobby Gillespie's clothing, for example, the kind of move that only Elvis Presley fans had previously been forced to endure. Collectors being what they are, the 'Riot' package quickly gained Holy Grail status, and currently changes hands for in excess of 50 quid. Fierce repeated the stunt with 'Searching For The Mary Chain', an album-length excursion into the riotous. And as their idea of a hero seems to be Charles Manson, further docu-drama J&MC releases cannot be ruled out.

WEA and The Mary Chain both spoke out against the 'Riot' single, sounding like the kind of music business veterans they had once been pledged to destroy. William hit a vein of truth, though, when he commented: "It's a dopey idea. Only dopes would buy it."

The second October 1985 single was the first indication that the band had decided to play their 'musical virtuosity' card. 'Just Like Honey' attracted instant calls of 'sell-out', from the kind of indie fans who couldn't adjust to more than one idea per decade. Musically, the detractors had no cause to complain – though the marketing of the single was less exemplary.

'Just Like Honey' saw The Mary Chain fall into the hands of WEA's publicity department. Just like the teeny bands they longed to accompany into the Top Ten, The Mary Chain were being promoted with multiple releases. The 7″ single included 'Head' on the B-side, while the 12″ added the ecstatic 'Cracked' and what claimed to be the original demo version of 'Just Like Honey'. Then there was a 7″ double-single package in a gatefold sleeve, which repeated the standard 7″ coupling, and added a second single, 'Cracked/Inside Me'. Both the double-pack and the 12″, you will note, included just one song unavailable on the other releases. Jesus And Mary Chain completists, already the proud owners of some of the shortest 12″ singles ever issued, now had to buy both configurations to keep their collections in shape. And WEA were only just beginning . . .

"To do a single again with noise on it would have been dull. It would have been predictable. Whereas 'Just Like Honey' has had the same effect that 'Upside Down' had – it's going to take everyone by surprise. To me, it's perfect, one hundred per cent The Jesus And Mary Chain."
(Jim Reid, November 1985.)

In place of the snarling feedback of the earlier singles, 'Just Like Honey' opened with a bass drum beat borrowed from an old Ronettes single like 'Be My Baby'. And the song came from a similar source – sounding more like a pop ballad than a foretaste of the apocalypse. William's guitars were still much in evidence, but providing a melodic drone rather than the dissonant wail of before. And Jim Reid's vocal was equally assured and controlled. It was a dramatic shift of emphasis in the band's approach, which boded well for the forthcoming début album.

Do It Again

▶

CHAPTER 8

While Warner Brothers moved into the marketing game, The Mary Chain suffered a personnel change. Drummer Bobby Gillespie had tired of finding his own career with Primal Scream subjugated to his part-time involvement with J&MC; as interviews revealed, Gillespie was a budding *enfant terrible* in his own right, quite able to satisfy a journalist's portable tape-recorder without mentioning the Reids, riots or feedback. In October 1985, he announced that he wanted out of The Mary Chain, and was going to devote himself to Primal Scream.

Gillespie's limited percussive ability was unlikely to be missed by Messrs Reid, Reid and Hart – his main strength had been his image. To assure that only the right applicants would consider the post, The Jesus And Mary Chain let slip that their new drummer would have to be "Familiar with Ginger Baker's drum solo on 'Toad'" – familiar enough to know that this 20-minute sonic barrage, one of sixties rock's least thrilling moments, had nothing in common with The Mary Chain's own approach. The jest won them valuable press space, and probably doubled Cream's royalties that week as 18-year-old drummers rushed to their local Our Price store to begin the familiarisation process.

By the time Gillespie left the band, recording sessions for their début album had been completed.– with John Moore stepping in whenever Gillespie had to be absent. A taster of the new recordings was unveiled shortly before the LP, in the form of 'Taste Of Cindy', one of four tracks featured on a free EP given away with the ill-fated young-male-lifestyle magazine *The Hit*. The Mary Chain's 95-second excursion into sonic powerplay was in bizarre contrast to the designer white soul of The Style Council, whose track preceded theirs on the disc.

The album followed in November. The title: 'Psychocandy'. "It's a good description of what the contents will be," explained Jim Reid helpfully. The album was the proverbial crossroads in the band's career. Punk had demonstrated how important a landmark a début long-player could be. Their début albums had proved The Sex Pistols to have written themselves out of material; and The Clash to have tapped a rich seam of subjects for lyrical annihilation.

The best début albums are the product of single-minded determination. They melt down a band's preoccupations into a narrow world-vision that sweeps all before it; they typify their sound at the same time as they represent the step forward into the unknown that they have taken. The classic débuts – 'Elvis

Presley', 'The Rolling Stones', 'The Velvet Underground And Nico', 'The Doors', Patti Smith's 'Horses', 'The Clash': all burn with a desire to be heard, to leave an indelible scar on the face of the earth while the chance is at hand. None of these records spread their net too far; they don't attempt stylistic virtuosity, leaving their experimentations into different fields for later records. The débuts say all that there is to say, on the assumption that there will never be another opportunity. On that level, 'Psychocandy' is as perfect a début album as you will ever hear.

It included the A-sides of the last three Mary Chain singles; but, as Andy Gill remarked in *New Musical Express*, "The way the singles slot in so comfortably here could make you think the album had dropped fully-formed from some celestial studio. Either every track on this LP is a single, or this group's an album band. Or both, which seems more like the case."

So 'Psychocandy' is not a diverse record, like The Beatles might have created, a comfortable mastery of stunningly different styles. Rather it sums up The Mary Chain's progress to date, and demonstrates that the furnace of their early singles was not kindled by accident. Feedback and simplicity are still at the heart of the band's sound, with almost every song creating an unbearable sonic tension, and then placing a fiercely controlled, almost emotionless vocal at the very heart of the inferno. The result was almost neurotic in its contrast. The multi-tracked guitar distortion constantly threatened to career uncontrollably off its supports and engulf the songs, which intoned their alienation and lack of feeling, apparently without being aware of the mania around them. Rarely has a record incited such violence, and then held it strictly under control.

"We've spent months doing remixes to get it just right. It's got to stand up for years. I hope it's going to be one of those LPs like the first Velvet Underground LP which always sells, everybody's got it and it's always in the shops. I'm trying to think of something like 20 years from now." (Jim Reid, November 1985.)

'Psychocandy' dispelled any ideas that The Mary Chain were anything less than *auteurs* of their own sound. Despite the image of random destruction created by their live shows, in the studio they were the masters of technology, crafting their aural extravaganzas out of numerous overdubs and constant remixing. William Reid's remarkable guitar noises were at the centre of every track but one; and again, what sounded in a casual listen like a single instrument feeding back was usually several quite separate feedback parts, melded into a carefully considered whole. "It's easy to record a song to sound as you wrote it," explained Jim Reid. "It's difficult to go into the studio and create a masterpiece, which is what we always try and do."

Just like the Reids promised, the album title was the *right* description of the band's music. It mixed the unpredictability of the psychopath with the sweetness, the transience of candy. The band's music conjured something that mattered out of an idiom that was pure throwaway, evoked emotional storms from the sweet repetition of early sixties song forms. 'Psychocandy' mixed the menace and the innocence that was The Mary Chain's trademark. What was remarkable about the record was that the innocence survived both the ravages of the band's sonic assault, and the studio craft that made it possible. The band might have been obscured by their own overdubs. Instead, they used the technology to create their message, rather than letting it control them.

The album opened with the *baion* beat of 'Just Like Honey', that unique mingling of Phil Spector's Wall of Sound and the seedy nihilism of the New York underground. It confirmed how far the band had come from the rampaging destruction of 'Upside Down'. In its place were a classic girl group melody, and structured layers of guitars, which gave the song a lingering beauty.

'The Living End' introduced a second strand of sixties influence – the surf guitar instrumental. 'Pipeline', originally recorded by the Chantays, summed up the era, with its deep, rumbling rhythms and unforgettable guitar riffs. The Mary Chain fed the surf style through the mixer, and emerged with a jagged antonym to the optimism of the sixties. Anyway, this song wasn't celebrating surf, but another sixties reference point, the motorbike. "Every LP should have a motorbike song," explained William Reid. "Ours is one where the hero gets his come-uppance. His head is dripping into his leather boots." And that's just how it sounds; the Shangri-Las' 'Leader Of The Pack', retold by the hero whose demise the Las' song describes.

'Taste The Floor' epitomised the control/aggression duel that litters the album. Surely it took an industrial lathe to create the hissing, explosive racket that was the song's instrumental track, while deep in the heart of the mix the band rehearsed some old Stooges riffs. Yet the simple three-note melody was cool, calm and collected, giving a feel of equilibrium to the frenzy of the white noise.

'The Hardest Walk' confirmed the band's mastery of pop history – from the updated Byrds jingle-jangle of the guitars, through the punky solo to the sudden break in the wall of feedback that allowed a simple bass/drum riff to take centre-stage, just like an old Ronettes record from 1963. But this was no honeydew romance; 'It's hard not to feel ashamed of the loving living games we play,' sang Reid, 'It's like a sick sick dream.' As Malcolm McLaren once asked, who killed Bambi?

'Cut Dead' was the album's token moment of peace – and its most obvious homage to The Velvet Underground. The Mary Chain had been constantly compared to The Velvets, though there were few overt similarities. But 'Cut Dead' made no excuses: its melody moved midway between 'Femme Fatale' and 'Sunday Morning' from The Velvets' own début, while the song had the same studied lack of emotion as Nico's vocals on that same album. The folk-rock tambourine and acoustic guitars were reminiscent of another mistress of emotional waste, Marianne Faithfull – a comparison that the lyrical accounts of sexual powerplay did little to resist.

'In A Hole' was the opposite extreme, a visit to the dentist's chair in which the drill doesn't stop at the gums. The song's four-chord homage to The Ramones was beside the point; what mattered was the noise, and more noise, and more noise. The sound said something that no lyrics could capture; lines like 'God spits on my soul' seemed like a bad parody of Black Sabbath rather than a summoning of ultimate evil.

'Taste Of Cindy' ended side one with its most obviously commercial ploy. Here some of the feedback drones sounded like distant horns, giving the track a vaguely psychedelic air. And although the lyrics made few concessions – 'Knife in my head is a taste of Cindy' – the sheer insistence of the song's second half gave it instant listener appeal. Had The Mary Chain wanted a slight dilution of their basic sound to improve their royalty statements, then 'Taste Of Cindy' would have been their weapon.

The second side began with the earblast of 'Never Understand', unchanged from the original single and, as Andy Gill had pointed out, sounding as it had been recorded on the same day as the rest of the album. Then came 'Inside Me', with all the usual ingredients – buzzsaw guitar, booming drums, and sheets of unbearable white noise. And there was another sly Velvets reference. Just as Lou Reed had prefaced his most extreme guitar solo with the words 'I felt my mind split open' (on 'I Heard Her Call My Name'), so Jim Reid introduced his brother's pyrotechnics with the line 'I felt my head expand.' There followed the aural equivalent of a Stephen King novel, all creeping horror and irresistible mental torment.

Like 'Just Like Honey', 'Sowing Seeds' opened with the *baion* beat (bom bom-bom) first popularised by The Drifters in the late fifties, and then a trademark of the Phil Spector sound. It presaged another more melodic, reflective song, which boasted that most unexpected of novelties, a change of key – which, after a side and a half of minimalist melodies, was as shocking as the most violent of feedback storms.

'My Little Underground' was pure Beach Boys, from its lyrical preoccupations – a hiding place for the soul, an answer to Brian Wilson's 'In My Room' – to the deceptively simple descending chord changes that underpinned the song. Play The Beach Boys fast and without finesse, and strip away the harmonies; and you sound just like The Ramones, which is what happened here. The Mary Chain attempted to hide the resemblance with a blazing feedback racket, and some random white noise creeping into gaps in the lyrics, but the comparison survived – only to be dissolved by the inclusion of another previous single, the anarchic 'You Trip Me Up'.

An album that had sacrificed melody on the altar of power closed with its two most simplistic melodies. 'Something's Wrong' boasted another majestic pastiche of the Phil Spector sound for openers, before running off the rails like a demented U2; while 'It's So Hard' stripped away all the band's meagre fineries, introduced the harshest feedback of the album, and repeated the same melodic phrase over and over. 'All of life is dreams' intoned Jim Reid, without explaining what kind he had in mind. The album ended with Reid's frantic screaming, echoed by his brother's infernal wall of feedback. Where the rest of the album swathed the promise of sixties idealism in eighties sound, leaving the outcome uncertain, 'It's So Hard' demolished any lingering optimism, and drove home a message of fear, hatred and disgust. It had to be the final track; there was no place else to go.

THE HISTORY
of **FEEDBACK**
PART ④

In the early 1970s, one of the original feedback pioneers indulged in a brief return to the fold. In 1969, Beatle John Lennon married Japanese conceptual artist Yoko Ono. Their partnership had already been documented on record with an album of random noise, dialogue and the sound of two people playing with a tape machine. Now they wanted to get serious.

Their second collaborative effort was 'Unfinished Music No. 2: Life With The Lions'. One side was filled with the debris of the hip avant-garde – two minutes' silence, the couple chanting their own press clippings, turning a radio on and off. The other documented a live appearance that the Lennons had granted to an arts festival at Cambridge University in February 1969.

Titled 'Cambridge 1969', it opened with Yoko Ono emitting a siren call that belonged to no musical key, followed by a 20-minute duet between Lennon's piercing feedback guitar and Ono's random vocal squeals. Lennon was entranced: here was music to tear down the Beatle barriers that had restricted him since 1962.

So it was that in 1970 John and Yoko recorded a matching pair of solo albums. Lennon's attempted to explain the process of Primal Therapy, the stripping away of memories to uncover the psychic pain that produced neurosis. Yoko needed no such instruction: she simply screamed her way to catharsis. On the opening track of her album, 'Why', the Lennons produced the ultimate synthesis of their backgrounds. Yoko yelled her lungs out; Klaus Voorman and Ringo Starr constructed a rock-hard rhythm section; and Lennon let rip with his guitar. After they had recorded six minutes of hard-rock psychotherapy, the Lennons listened to the tapes, and found that in places they couldn't tell the feedback from the vocals.

Amusement Parks USA

▶

CHAPTER 9

With 'Psychocandy' happily ensconced as one of the greatest rock LPs of all time, The Mary Chain set out to conquer the New World. The American music scene is broader-minded than *Billboard* charts and MTV videos might suggest. The lack of any national indie chart, or credible 'underground' music paper with coast-to-coast circulation, tends to underemphasise the strength of the left-field alternative in a country that is better able to cope with non-conformism than some of its smaller transatlantic contemporaries.

This failure in underground communication means that America is spared the elitist faddism which benumbs the British indie scene. In the UK, you fall into step when the cultural arbiters speak, or run the risk of being ridiculed or – even worse – ignored. Britain is small enough for a handful of weekly journals to invent trends, and make their more susceptible readers feel as if they are missing out. Only the strict British desire to belong can account for some of the more absurd bandwagons which have been rolled over the music press in the last decade.

America reacts more slowly to the currents of fashion, and in the mainstream the audience is manipulated more openly than in Britain. But beneath the glitter and gloss of MTV videos is a genuine acceptance of experimentation, of honest endeavour in any field, no matter how unhip it seems. And although Americans individually are less in love with the British accent than the cliché might have you believe, since The Beatles there has been an awareness that the UK might conceivably produce a movement that could transform mainstream American culture.

Once again, we're back to the coast-to-coast dilemma. Unless you crack the mainstream, you have to convert the country a city at a time. The Sex Pistols attempted to subvert the process by creating national news stories; but they were never offered the shot at the Johnny Carson Show that might have allowed them the chance. Similarly, it was naïve to expect that the J&MC, purveying a genuinely revolutionary sound that would not translate well to prime-time TV, would suddenly turn up on NBC, ABC or CBS in front of a national audience.

But the American *cognoscenti* were sufficiently well primed by their diet of British papers to recognise a phenomenon when they saw one, and – to their credit – the head office of the mighty Warner Brothers corporation did their best to publicise The Mary Chain's Stateside adventure, taking full-page ads in the trades to announce the release of 'Psychocandy'. The band were still a long way from selling out Madison Square Garden or Shea Stadium, however: late December 1985 and early January 1986 saw them touring small clubs along the East Coast of America, before spreading their horizons to California, home of a local brand of post-punk that suggested The Mary Chain might find the visit congenial.

As usual, American journalists remained more difficult to convince. Charles Dodson, stringer for the London paper *Sounds*, spent a delightful New Year's Eve in The Mary Chain's company, enduring a gig in one of the bastions of white R&B, Boston, Massachusetts. "Life's cruelties never cease," began his scathing report on the latest British invasion. "While people are falling down drunk across town, I am condemned to endure an embarrassing romp through feedback land; 40 minutes of music that's bound to set rock 'n' roll back to, oh, 1977." He condemned Jim Reid's 'fucks' and brother William's guitar chords, before asking: "These are the new Sex Pistols?" Well, no, actually, but carry on . . . "J&MC are just another angry night dressed in black, a laconic theatre-of-the-absurd, an embarrassment to the spirit of Sid. The Pistols at least threw melody into their madness. 'Upside Down' and 'Never Understand', on the other hand, are merely noise disguised as histrionics."

"An embarrassment to the spirit of Sid?" It's difficult to imagine anything more embarrassing than Sid himself, shambling through another display of self-mutilation in the belief that he was changing anything apart from his skin texture. In America, The Mary Chain were suddenly faced with their *bête noire*, The Sex Pistols comparison. It had taken months to drag the British press (and manager McGee) away from the idea of a Pistols revival; now they had to do it all over again. Despite the example posed by homegrown bands like Hüsker Dü and Sonic Youth, most American critics were unable to relate to The Mary Chain without remembering The Pistols. First time around, the US didn't appreciate The Pistols until it was too late. This time, they were taking no chances. It was just a shame that The Mary Chain were playing an entirely different ballgame.

THE HISTORY
***of* FEEDBACK**
PART ⑤

Lou Reed spent his time after The Velvet Underground dabbling with drugs, drug imagery and quirky pop songs. Only on 'Berlin' did he come close to the artistic force of The Velvets' records, by conjuring up the sound and spirit of decadent pre-war Germany. To complete his contract with RCA, he recorded a double-album called 'Metal Machine Music'–either a masterpiece of the avant-garde, or the ultimate raised finger to his record company. Or, quite conceivably, both.

The album comprises four sides of varying tone, recorded at deafening volume. Reed provided lavish technical details on the sleeve, for anyone who cared to copy him. 'Metal Machine Music' is by no means as unlistenable as its initial detractors complained, but it is unlikely to appeal to anyone impressed by the arch smuttiness of 'Walk On The Wild Side'. But it proves that noise – atonal, arhythmic, random – has a meaning and a tempo of its own; without being attractive, it can be beautiful. 'Metal Machine Music' is not even aggressive: it merely reproduces the daily working environment of the world's factory-hands, and offers it up as entertainment. Previous experiments with noise and feedback had all been compromised by melody, or sabotaged by pretension. Reed's hour-long metallic rasp made no concessions on any level. It will age only when industry eliminates noise.

Kraftwerk

Reed's example was already being imitated in Germany, where industrial noise was apparently a national preoccupation. German bands like Can, Faust and Kraftwerk have all taken random noise, processed it, and forced it into accompanying minimalist melodies. The eerie drone of what became known (racistly) as Kraut-Rock became a familiar presence in the British underground movement, as an antidote to the technical flourishes and Aeolian cadences of the classically-inspired progressive rockers. Unfortunately, the Euro-rockers performed their music in robotic style, a stance taken to its ultimate absurdity by the unfortunate Gary Numan. With Germany's modern history in mind, rock critics were all too willing to dismiss their controlled, neurotic presentation as 'fascist'.

Few of the German bands put noise to any constructive use, however. Merely to have discovered the noise was, it seemed, sufficient. Even Einsturzende Neubaten, the most uncompromising German exponents of noise, were unable to find a purpose for their racket. The band attracted much attention in Britain early in the eighties for their live appearances, which saw them taking industrial music to its final conclusions. Rather than using computers to recreate the sounds of industry, they used the industrial equipment itself. So it was that avant-garde audiences thrilled to the sight of pneumatic drills and heavy anvils being wielded on stage, with all the panache of a rock rebel posing with his Stratocaster. The initial effect was startling, not to say discomforting. But on record, Einsturzende Neubaten were reduced to the last refuge of the avant-garde – occasional 'found sounds' accompanying pretentious poetry. The immediacy of the music was undercut by the prissiness of the intention, and Einsturzende merely became another ghetto-ised, elitist vanguard of a movement without followers.

Lou Reed

Busy Doin' Nothing
▶
CHAPTER 10

With their début American visit under their belts, and 'Psychocandy' creeping around the bottom reaches of the *Billboard* Top 200 Albums chart, The Mary Chain moved on briefly to the world's second biggest record-buying market – Japan. As yet, the Land of the Rising Sun has not fallen under The Mary Chain's spell; we still await the double live set 'The Jesus And Mary Chain Live At The Budokan'.

Then it was back to Britain, for what – remarkably – was the band's longest British tour to date. Within a fortnight they played eight gigs in Aberdeen, Glasgow, Sheffield, Coventry, Blackburn, Norwich, Liverpool and Nottingham – a good old-fashioned excursion of the type that most superstar bands had abandoned years ago. But the tour passed without incident. Trouble was kept to a minimum; audiences refused to riot when The Mary Chain limited their sets to half-an-hour; and, because the tour didn't reach London, the national music press ignored it.

1986, a strange year in the band's history, saw them haunted by rumour and oppressed by public expectations. The Reids had arrived on the scene as rock 'n' roll revolutionaries, destroying in order to create. The backlash which greeted their early publicity hype had drained them of some of their ebullience, and during 1985 the Reid brothers began to sound less like carefree punks and more like conscience-bearers for a generation. In interviews, the group displayed none of the brash self-confidence of the early Beatles, Stones or Pistols. Jim Reid dominated the conversation, but he spoke slowly, almost wearily, choosing his words with care, as if media minefields were waiting to trap any unwary statement. His brother William perched uneasily on the outskirts of the conversation. Drummer Gillespie was apt to take over proceedings if allowed to mention his own pet project, Primal Scream; while Douglas Hart was rarely quoted at all.

Something of the brothers' pre-J&MC isolation in Scotland hung over William Reid. While his brother at least revelled in the band's stage performances, William found each part of the pop process forbidding. "I hate doing interviews because the real me never comes across," he confessed during a break in his brother's philosophical musings. "I always get tongue-tied and slightly stuttered and shy. An interview, to me, is like being on the psychiatrist's couch, except it's not just between me and the psychiatrist, it's between me and 200,000 people, and when I start to think of that, I feel embarrassed.

"Over in Belgium, we did a TV interview and I just froze. The guy was asking me a question and I just looked at him, trying to get away with giving him my psychotic stare, trying to look mysterious, but I was really totally fucking embarrassed. I also hate it when I do interviews and what I say gets credited to Jim. That makes my life just a wee bit more miserable. It's a happy day when one of his gets credited to me."

Jim was equally thoughtful when confronted in this period. Words were something he was never short of, but communication remained an unsolved problem. "I have a terrible fear of being misunderstood," he revealed in November 1985. "Maybe it is paranoia, but I get the impression that our group has been completely misunderstood. It does have a lot to do with our own naïvety, because we created a stupid image which we're finding it very hard to get rid of. But when I do an interview I want to describe everything that the band are doing, everything that we're trying to be – but there are no easy words."

The struggle to be heard was perhaps one reason why the band opted for a shift in sound during their sparse 1986 recordings. The process had begun in the previous autumn. The band, remember, had toyed with the idea of playing acoustic gigs in support of Sonic Youth. Stymied with this plan, they transferred the experiment to the radio waves.

John Peel's show, an early champion of the band, was the obvious venue for the acoustic outing. (The loyalty of the show's audience was demonstrated at the end of the year, when the J&MC dominated the listeners' choice of Peel's *Festive Fifty* for 1985, rivalled only by the antithesis of their approach, The Smiths.) That November, the band recorded a four-track Peel session – creating music that their previous recordings had only hinted at.

'Cut Dead' represented the safest entry to this new Mary Chain sound. On the 'Psychocandy' album, it was the softest track, the easiest arrangement on the ear, with its echoes of folk-rock and the Nico-led Velvet Underground. For the Peel show, the band stripped down the album arrangement still further, with acoustic guitars that jangled across each other, vaguely out of key; a rattling tambourine; and only Douglas Hart's bass, way down in the mix, to remind the world of the band's electric origins. The slightly tuneless, decadent sound that resulted was a throwback to vintage Stones – to an obscure flipside called 'The Singer Not The Song', in fact, where producer Andrew Oldham had allowed Keith Richard and Brian Jones to detune their guitars to the point where the song only just held together. Given the Reids' Stones fixation, the resemblance can't have been accidental.

'You Trip Me Up' also received the minimalist treatment; it says much for its strength and structure that the song retained all its haunting power, even without the riveting feedback that had apparently been its mainspring. The acoustic version was eerie, in fact, with guitars jangling almost out of earshot, and all the emphasis thrown on the basic rhythm and relentless vocal. The guitar solo proved William Reid's mastery of his instrument. It was delicate, totally acoustic – yet played with a spirit that was much closer to rock 'n' roll than folk.

Two new songs were premièred on this Peel show. One was 'Psychocandy', the album title track that was then omitted from the LP. In this version it was listless, with a drum part that sounded as if it had been played on a suitcase – exactly, in fact, like Maureen Tucker's work with (them again!) The Velvet Underground. And the words! 'The world is spreading its strange disease for my psycho candy . . . she'll take the pointed sharpened blade and give you something warm to taste . . . and the world is turning round and on and on and on . . . for my psycho candy.'

Back in 1966, when The Magic Mushrooms announced 'It's All Happening', they described how 'The world is turning round and round and round . . . ' and they weren't talking about the revolutions of the earth around the sun. Similarly, the Mary Chain's 'Candy' seemed to have a chemical origin. Commented Jim Reid several months later: "To explain lyrics defeats them, as if they're not good enough to stand up as lyrics or poetry or whatever. I can deny 'Psychocandy' is about acid, but that's all I'll say."

The fourth song on the Peel session repeated the 'candy' reference, and eventually turned it into a crusade. For now, though, 'Some Candy Talking' was just another song – one which the band had been performing for almost a year, but which they had had the foresight to leave off their début album. As the radio version proved, the song was their strongest to date, with a tight, coherent structure. The band kept to the acoustic guitar/tambourine format of the rest of the session, while William Reid contributed another studied solo. The atmosphere built gently towards the end, but it was a kiss, not a punch.

For the moment, the song aroused no controversy. The Peel session was aired; the band's supporters duly noted their idols' versatility, and then sat back to enjoy the full-scale thrust of the 'Psychocandy' album.

Two months later, *New Musical Express* issued a free single with one of their weekly issues. As part of the *NME*'s 'Big Four', The Mary Chain sat alongside tracks by Trouble Funk, Hüsker Dü and Tom Waits. All four acts offered slightly oblique perspectives on their music: The Mary Chain served up a work in progress, in the shape of an early electric recording of 'Some Candy Talking'. This second version of the song was faster, almost too hurried; but it retained the basic jingle-jangle of the acoustic track, merely translating it into an electric format. And this time, when Jim Reid whispered 'talk', William's guitar solo was harsh and urgent, moving the song into a new dimension. Like the massed strings that took the solos on old Drifters records from the late fifties, his guitar offered an emotional release that the rest of the song couldn't quite capture. And *NME* readers being, in the main, broad-minded souls, the song's lyrics once again raised no eyebrows.

In June 1986, The Jesus And Mary Chain announced plans for another British tour. Days later, it was scrapped. Organisational difficulties were blamed at first, before rumours spread that Jim Reid – not his more obviously unhappy brother – had suffered a nervous breakdown. This was amended to the more acceptable 'exhaustion' by the band's management.

The release of a new single in July, their first new record of the year, effectively masked the band's personal problems. Completing a trio of recorded versions, the A-side was 'Some Candy Talking'; and this time the nation's moral guardians were listening to the words. The single had already enjoyed substantial (for The Mary Chain) BBC airplay when disc jockey and professional young person Mike Smith, taking time off from building his own career as a safe media personality, an ersatz Noel Edmunds, declared on air that 'Candy' was a paean to illegal drugs, and that he would be asking the Beeb to ban the single from further airplay. The BBC didn't tell Smith to mind his own business; remembering their current unpopularity among government ministers, and the nationwide anti-heroin campaign, they confessed their sins in scenes reminiscent of the Stalinist purges of the 1930s, and The Mary Chain were, if not formally banned, at least placed on an unofficial list of material unsuitable for broadcast to impressionable minors.

The Mary Chain were immediately transformed into libertarian heroes. They denied the charges, suggesting instead that words like 'candy' and 'cindy' had a melodious ring that made them obvious subjects for lyric writing. The music press had a field day at Mike Smith's expense: the video had been shown on *Top Of The Pops*, and the song still made the Top 20.

The irony, of course, was that Smith was right. "Everybody was talking about how it was a drug song," remembered William Reid a year later, "advocating drugs or whatever. And we said, 'Don't be ridiculous, we never had that in mind at all.' But, reading the lyric, it *is* a drug song. It's just a pure drug song. All the words, 'I'm going down to the place tonight, so I can get a taste tonight,' it's just a pure drug lyric. We hotly denied it at the time, though, but I forgive everybody, I own up to it."

The media discussion effectively subdued objective analysis of the record – which was quite simply a masterpiece. The single version of 'Some Candy Talking' took all the promise of the earlier recordings, and fulfilled it. Stabbing guitar flourishes were added to the intro, while the song's structure was heightened with dramatic guitar breaks, pounding drum beating

(four to the bar, just like The Velvets) and a vocal that even hinted at (gasp!) Bruce Springsteen. For The Mary Chain, this was their most mainstream move to date – though it was achieved without compromising any of their original power or majesty. The band's ambition had been to create the perfect pop record: 'Some Candy Talking' was their closest shot yet.

The 7" single featured two songs on the B-side. The first was an electric reworking of 'Psychocandy', very simple and very controlled, all the time perched on the edge of a dramatic release of tension. In a way, this fuller arrangement was even gentler than the acoustic version; it was certainly another mark of the band's total command of the studio.

'Hit' completed a trilogy of songs with lyrics that reflected drug experiences. Its rumbling, menacing guitar textures underpinned Jim Reid's repeated vocal cries, while feedback stalked through the song like a Stephen King creation. The band once again summoned up industrial white noise, but rather than allowing the noise to control the structure, they caged it within a steady rock beat, making the results even more threatening.

In the recent WEA tradition, two further variations of the single were released. On the 12", the band included an acoustic 'Taste Of Cindy', similar in effect to their previous acoustic ventures. And there was also a limited double-pack single, that coupled the orthodox 7" single with a partner which included all four of the acoustic Peel tracks. As such, it represented the peak of The Mary Chain's development so far – acoustic and electric readings of the same dream. 'Some Candy Talking' may have been the band's only new release in 1986, but it attained a level of perfection that made their subsequent silence easier to bear.

THE HISTORY *of* **FEEDBACK** **PART** ⑥ While Britain and Germany played with noise, America put it to use. In the early eighties, California and Minnesota gave birth to hardcore – a music that took the raw aggression of punk, stripped away its quirkier English edges, and catapulted the results at an array of all-American targets from mother-love to the President. At first, their attitude was more important than their sound; the sheer fact of Americans making this anti-social racket was the event, not what they were saying.

But as hardcore, like any musical form, matured and developed, so the pioneers of modern American noise began to broaden their line of fire. Bands like X, Sonic Youth and the Minutemen combined cascades of molten feedback with searing lyrical analysis of America's complacency; and across the heartlands, scores of young musicians heard the call.

But it was Hüsker Dü from Minneapolis who perfected the new feedback. Their music had a seamless power that carried all before it. They played at deafening volume, which in person robbed their sound of the emotional commitment that gave it strength. On record, however, they were awesome, both with their material and with a succession of classic covers. The Beatles were favourite targets for their love-hate deconstruction course. But it was those previous masters of the atonal guitar, The Byrds, who were on the receiving end of the decade's most intense feedback assault. In 1983, Hüsker Dü recorded 'Eight Miles High'. The song was swept aside in a rush of screaming vocals and irrepressible guitar, as the band abandoned the lyrics in favour of an incoherent roar of passion and pain.

Someone sat the song's original composer, Gene Clark, in a darkened room with Hüsker Dü's record. He emerged baffled but impressed – and unable to recognise the mutant growth of his own creation.

Surf's Up
▶
CHAPTER 11

The Mary Chain had similar ambitions. First, though, there was the small matter of a career to manage. Between the release of 'Some Candy Talking' and the end of 1986, The Jesus And Mary Chain lost their manager, came close to splitting up, and finally managed to perform on two consecutive nights in London without causing a riot.

Drummer John Moore had made his live début with the group at the Hammersmith Palais earlier in the year. By the autumn, he had become the group's second guitarist, while former Redskin Martin Hewes took over the drumstool.

Other changes happened at the same time. It had become increasingly apparent that The Mary Chain had diverged from the *agit-pop* tactics of manager Alan McGee – himself preoccupied with the major label status of Primal Scream, and the recording career of his personal obsession, Biff! Bang! Pow! – and had elected to ignore his sensationalistic publicity campaigns in favour of their own more restrained approach. It was not a major surprise, then, when the band announced in September 1986 that they were no longer under McGee's aegis. In the true independent spirit of the band, the J&MC proclaimed that they were now being managed by Jim Reid's French girlfriend Lauren – who was probably capable of playing a bash-for-bash copy of Ginger Baker's drum solo on 'Toad' as well.

Sanity prevailed by the end of the year, and the group appointed Geoff Travis as their manager. He already ran their label, Blanco y Negro, as well as their stablemates, Everything But The Girl, and also had some degree of command over Rough Trade Records. Given the Reids' recent work-rate, however, he probably reckoned that adding the band to his managerial roster wouldn't keep him up too late at nights.

In November 1986, rumours spread through the London pop press that the band were on the verge of a split. Jim Reid had, remember, been officially 'exhausted' in the summer; his brother William sounded equally jaded; and no-one else in the group ever said a word. The band had apparently found 1986 a year of taking stock, more draining than the 12 months of bedlam which had preceded it. By the time the group surfaced for interviews, no-one was talking about a split, and there was no hint of a rift between the brothers. If it wasn't for the fact that he had just been sacked, one might have suspected the dread hand of Alan McGee's publicity machine hoping to stir fresh interest in the otherwise moribund band.

To confirm that the band were still in working order, they appeared at the National Ballroom in Kilburn, North London, on December 15 and 16 1986. The dual guitar assault allowed them to come closer to the multi-dubbed textures of their studio work than their previous line-up; and The Mary Chain used the occasion to unveil some new songs. 'April Skies' was officially launched during these gigs, together with a haunting ballad called 'Don't Get Hit'. And the group's Rolling Stones fixation moved a little closer to the surface with a churning cover version of Bo Diddley's 'Mona', a staple of the Stones' earliest live shows.

After Christmas, the band returned to the studio, to begin serious work on a follow-up to the 'Psychocandy' album. "We started to get screwed up about not wanting to sound the same," explained Jim Reid later in the year, "and that was a problem. It was so obvious what we were trying to do on 'Psychocandy' that I knew what it was going to sound like before we'd done it. This time it wasn't clear what it was going to end up like. So we were chipping away at each other's ideas all the time, and we recorded totally different versions of some of the songs."

The band's first completed tracks from the second album sessions appeared in April, with the release of the 'April Skies' single. Once again, Warner Brothers worked overtime, with no apparent complaint from the group – who evidently expected their fans to buy the 7", 12" and 7" double-pack variations that were thrown into the shops. Someone obviously did; by May the single had reached number eight in the Gallup charts, establishing The Jesus And Mary Chain as *bona fide* pop stars.

And it couldn't have happened to a finer record (except, perhaps, 'Some Candy Talking'!). 'April Skies' marked another definite step away from the transcendent anti-commercialism of their early singles – and another root into the riches of rock's 30-year tradition. Expertly produced by William Reid and Bill Price, the record surged around a classic chugging guitar rhythm, beloved of every rock group from The Stones onwards. The melody was made to match, keeping close to

The Mary Chain's favourite chord changes, but with some subtle twists to keep The Velvets comparisons at bay. And just like 'Candy Talking', the song showed that the band were masters of dynamics, of creating a tension and slowly tightening it until the structure was fit to burst.

Once again, the band built towards a climax and then let it slip away, always maintaining control. On the 7″ version the song ended on repeated choruses; 12″ purchasers were rewarded with a third, short verse before the close. Lyrically, the song had none of the ambivalence of 'Some Candy Talking'– unless you chose to believe that the Reids loved nothing but their drugs. This time the subject was romance – though hardly the moon-and-June clichés of the Glasgow soul bands: 'Hand in hand in a violent life/Making love on the edge of a knife . . . I'm going back for the good of my health.' And the music had all the coiled passion of the imagery.

"When it comes to a boy meets girl situation I'm not in the least bit romantic. Romantic to me means that you build up an idea of something and nothing touches it. I tend to get romantic about things like the Hells Angels, you know, motorbikers that wear dirty black leather. They're good-looking, sit on Harley-Davidson motorcycles, they don't fart, they definitely don't fart. That to me is romance. People are too complex to get romantic about. I'm romantic about rock 'n' roll music. To me rock 'n' roll is a very romantic area."
(Jim Reid, September 1987.)

The Beach Boys may not have invented surf music, but they perfected it. Brian Wilson, the group's erratic leader and composer, married the three-chord simplicity of rock 'n' roll to the effortless harmonies of the Four Freshmen, and created a blend of melody and rhythm previously unimagined in popular music. Having begun his writing career with pale pastiches of pre-rock ballads, he struggled for a subject until his brother, Beach Boys drummer Dennis Wilson, suggested he write songs about the teenage obsession of Southern California – surf. Guitarist Dick Dale had already pioneered the rhythms and reverbed guitar technique at the heart of the surf sound; Brian Wilson gave it meaning, and created a Californian legend.

One of Wilson's earliest hits was 'Surf City', written for surf duo Jan and Dean (although it was Wilson's own fragile falsetto that sold the record). In this song, he constructed a male paradise – sun, surf, hot rods, and 'two girls for every boy.' For two further years, Brian Wilson and The Beach Boys refined that myth – until Wilson found the strains of being a composer, performer, singer, musician, producer and all-round genius too much to bear, retired to his room, and relied less on the sea for his stimulation than on the contents of his medicine cabinet.

The Beach Boys performed these two-minute tales of teenage love, lust and liberty in strict uniform – candy-striped shirts and white trousers – that were at odds with the band's backstage dramas of drugs and debauchery. As their music progressed, so the image became all the more difficult to stomach. Jim Reid: "I think the whole surf thing had a lot of potential . . . I mean, think of The Beach Boys – brilliant songs, but look at the way they dressed, look at the way they produced their records. It should have been a gang of Hells Angels that made surf music."

On the flipside of 'April Skies', The Mary Chain set about another rewriting of image and history. 'Kill Surf City' was a blatant copy of Wilson's song; but then Wilson himself had borrowed the structure and melody of Chuck Berry's 'Sweet Little Sixteen' for his own 'Surfin' USA' without batting an eyelid. The Mary Chain's rendition didn't just transform surf music, it destroyed it; but the monster had puppy love in its eyes.

The track burst open with sixties motorbike sounds, and howls of feedback, before a relentless drum machine kicked Wilson's melody into life. The new words were lost in the hail of noise, with a screeching guitar taking the place of Brian Wilson's original falsetto. But odd phrases crept through the daze, offering images of death and hate. And as the guitars built in intensity, so the threat of the song's title came to pass. After a solo of random noise, with voices from a radio fighting for breath amidst a flurry of hissing guitars, the song degenerated into a nightmarish sound collage, with only the drum machine keeping the structure alive, until that too blipped feebly into silence.

" 'Kill Surf City' is a classic, you know," William Reid insisted. "It doesn't matter if it sounds like The Beach Boys or Jan and Dean. It's like every good surf song stuck into one package. The words are quite bizarre because they go against the grain of the usual surf song." And he added a warning for purists of other genres: "We're thinking of doing an LP like 'Kill Surf City', sort of taking styles of music and doing what we did to 'Kill Surf City'. We're thinking of doing it but I don't know if we're gonna have the time."

For the moment, the band were content to restrict their assaults. On the 12″ single of 'April Skies', the band added a cover version of Bo Diddley's 'Who Do You Love', but although the results were powerful, with a fuzz guitar pulsing throughout the track like a refugee from a sixties garage band, the track was gentle by comparison with the ritual dismembering of 'Surf City'. Still, making Bo Diddley sound like an honorary member of The Velvet Underground was entertainment enough.

The canonisation of Bo Diddley continued on the free record included in the 7″ double-pack release. 'Bo Diddley Is Jesus' announced the Reids, before letting loose their standard uptempo feedback snarl on a riff of dubious heritage. On the other side, The Mary Chain unearthed a live recording from the previous year – a cover of Can's 'Mushroom' (from the 'Tago Mago' double set), recorded – suitably enough – in Nuremburg. The song could have been written for The Mary Chain, with its repetitions and lazy two-chord melody, and all the J&MC had to do to customise the arrangement was add the expected feedback hail. 'Mushroom' added another cultural symbol to the band's Candy store, and ensured that their repertoire of cover versions retained its pedigree.

Shut Down

▶

CHAPTER 12

"That's us, the Lennon and McCartney of the eighties. Actually, we've always been fucked up by that, we thought we were wonderful songwriters and everybody would recognise that, but nobody's taken us that way. People have focused on the guitars and the way the records were so out of the ordinary, rather than considering the songs. We don't make records until there's something to record. I think a lot of people go into the studio with a producer, a few half-baked ideas and bash something out. What's really bad about that is that it works, it's successful for those people. You hear records that obviously haven't got a song but God knows how many people are raving about it. That's kinda sad."
(Jim Reid, August 1987.)

'April Skies' had been The Mary Chain's biggest hit to date – ironically at a time when they found themselves increasingly at odds with the machinations of the rock business. In a way, they had been more acceptable to the establishment as feedback-crazed anarchists than they were in their new guise of pop craftsmen. In 1987, the accepted way to make a hit record was to string together an image and a chord progression, conjure up the remnants of an old Tamla tune and then call in a succession of name producers and engineers to remix it into the charts. The weekly rock press were predictably unimpressed – though they proved to be equally gullible in different directions.

It was a year when white rock critics were going through one of their customary guilt-ridden bouts of positive discrimination. White music was in the doldrums; therefore black music was wonderful. Never mind that black music might be equally stultifying and predictable; it had an authentic air of the street. So, for rock writers at least, 1987 was the year of hip-hop and rap; and suddenly anyone who could string together a sexist rant about their own ego was a counter-culture hero. Critics were also overwhelmed by 'sampling', the technique whereby producers stole the work of others, and cut it together with extracts from commercials, film soundtracks, politicians' speeches, animal noises – whatever.

It should have been invigorating; but a fool with a tape machine is a fool nonetheless, and little of the hip-hop that dominated the weekly press was interesting on more than a theoretical level. But it was new, and to an industry that thrived on the appearance of novelty, that was all-important.

Where did that leave The Jesus And Mary Chain? They were nearly three years into their recording career, and impaled on the horns of a dilemma. If they merely repeated their early triumphs, they would be herded into a commercial ghetto – and face accusations that they were a one-idea group. If they changed – in any way moderated their stance – then they would be deemed to have sold out. They choose the latter course anyway, and the critical backlash duly followed.

Meanwhile, another new single consolidated their new sound. 'Happy When It Rains' appeared in August 1987; and like 'April Skies', it was very much a piece of craftsmanship rather than spontaneity. If anything, it was even more mainstream than its predecessor, hinged around a slow, Stones-like riff, and with a majestic structure that wouldn't have been out of place on a U2 album. The song ebbed and flowed across the same chord changes for three minutes, and Jim Reid added his lightest and most playful vocal to date.

Lyrically, the song updated Smokey Robinson's classic 'My Girl'. Where Smokey had declared 'I got sunshine on a cloudy day/ When it's cold outside I got the month of May,' the Reids inverted the metaphor, and gave it frightening connotations. Jim Reid found himself 'Looking at me enjoying something that feels like pain' and the same masochistic imagery ran through the lyric, from 'I would shed my skin for you' to 'She can take my darkest feeling/Tear it up till I'm on my knees'; and you knew he was loving every minute.

The flipside, 'Everything's Alright When You're Down', returned to an older style. Like some songs on the first album, it surrounded an old Pistols riff with feedback, and then dug into a tune left over from a sixties hot rod album. And for the chorus, the Reids borrowed the middle eight of The Monkees' 'You Just May Be The One', a sly reference to their influences that most observers would have missed.

No fewer than three other editions of the single appeared. The 10″ version added the rather nondescript 'Shake', plus a demo version of the A-side, which simply showed how much the Reids were in command of the studio. The 12″ had a longer version of the A-side, achieved by repeating the title phrase a few more times, and added 'Happy Place', a great pop song that had hints of The Turtles from the sixties and The Buzzcocks

from the seventies in its melodic twists and turns. And at the end of the 12″ B-side was 'F-Hole', about a minute of beautifully rendered rain noises pasted with uncompromising feedback. Finally, a limited edition boxed 7″ single not only contained J&MC postcards, but also a different track listing to the normal single – though with no new material.

'Happy When It Rains' was, somewhat surprisingly, a comparative failure, only reaching the nether regions of the Top Thirty. Airplay was still the band's problem; they were alienating old fans without being exposed to new ones, and as pop radio became increasingly vacuous, and more a vehicle for personalities than music, so their difficulties would increase.

The band finally achieved what had once seemed impossible at the start of September 1987, when they set out on a full-scale British tour. Previous attempts had been blighted by illness, bans or simply ennui. By Bruce Springsteen's standards, their September excursion was hardly strenuous, although the band now doubled the average length of their set to 45 minutes.

To no-one's great surprise, the music press greeted the event with indifference; former J&MC champions *New Musical Express* described the group as "The new Dire Straits." No more damning epitaph could be imagined.

"Onstage, we're one of the sexiest groups you can imagine. Three or four reasonably young guys in leather rolling around showing their backsides to the audience. All I know is that we get tons of screaming young girls. If a gig doesn't have sex there's something wrong. We're not pin-ups, but you don't have to be to be sexy. Some of our shows have been fantastic, we look exactly how groups should look. Groups shouldn't look sober or stand at the mikes and sing. Singers should roll on the ground and kick guitars."
(Jim Reid, August 1987.)

"I've never felt comfortable onstage, never. Playing live is the biggest contradiction. Everything we do in the studio may sound spontaneous, but it's not, it takes time. I've always hated other people's songs played live too. I just hate gigs.

JMC

"When I go on tour I just become a zombie, I can't do anything a normal human being can. I can't get any grasp of a thread of humanity. Don't try and tell me it's any better than sitting at home and watching TV. You don't even get different types of food, you just get the same old shit."
(William Reid, August 1987.)

The Reid brothers' ambivalent attitude to touring was a preoccupation in the autumn of 1987. Interviewers noticed a change in the pair's approach, a more thoughtful, less confident stance. For all his earlier exhaustion, Jim Reid revelled in the concert arena, in the exaggerated showmanship that had been the staple of rock 'n' roll from the days of Elvis Presley and Jerry Lee Lewis onwards. William, meanwhile, grew to hate the entire touring experience.

Jim noted: "He's definitely withdrawn since we started the group. He's become a recluse and I've become the pushy one. He never goes to gigs or pubs or any sort of parties, nothing. He just sits in the house and does absolutely nothing, or phones you up and has totally depressing conversations about how he's gonna kill himself.

"We've been all over the world and seen many strange and wonderful cities. All he sees is different hotels and TV sets. We had 10 days' holiday in Los Angeles and I don't think he and his girlfriend left the hotel room once." While Jim kept his eye open for a party, William watched out for potential muggers, or homosexual rapists.

Britain ought to have proved a less terrifying terrain than the States, but even this UK venture had its drawbacks, as Jim Reid remarked when the tour was over: "The British tour was weird because it was the first thing we did for a year and a half. At Portsmouth, getting onstage was quite scary. And it was weird playing with a drum machine. But by the time we got to Europe, we were more confident and felt like we were in control."

Ah yes, playing with a drum machine. Filling the fourth quarter of The Jesus And Mary Chain proved an impossible task, once Bobby Gillespie had opted for Primal Scream instead of drummerhood. Various drummers had been considered for the

role, but the job basically involved doing what you were told by Jim and William Reid, and an electronic drummer seemed the least likely to answer back. At the same time, it restricted the band's onstage momentum – and also gave their music a spirit of lifelessness at the core that worked against their emotional intensity.

As the machine-led Mary Chain toured Britain, and then fortunate parts of the Continent, their second album reached the shops. 'Darklands' was immaculately packaged as ever, with atmospheric stills from their recent videos placed within the band's customary design of red and black. The cover fitted the title; and so did the music.

Two years after 'Psychocandy', the band had produced a 10-song album – with two tracks that had already appeared on singles. Faced with the question of why the album took so long to complete, Jim Reid had no shame: "Why shouldn't it? Do people not think it's strange how everybody in the music business writes the same amount of songs each year? They do it because it's what's expected, so they get their advance. That's why so many LPs only have about four good songs and the rest is filler. We could have done that but if you're going to do something you should think about it and take time over it."

The album certainly had the air of a statement. It was certainly less extreme than the début, less of a revolution of the mind, to quote James Brown. But then nothing could have equalled the impact of 'Psychocandy', or have captured the same element of surprise. 'Darklands' was always going to be a more considered record; what mattered was what the band had left to say, and how they would say it.

The title track provided some clues. One of three songs to feature lead vocals by William Reid, rather than his brother, it established that the pair's world vision was identical. Like the band's recent singles, 'Darklands' had a rich, cavernous and stately sound, at once romantic and tragic; and William's heartfelt vocals gave the thinly metaphorical lyrics a real power. The song is hinged around the simplest of rhythm guitar parts, and was constructed with a real elegance and wit.

Humour, in fact, was the only plausible explanation for one of the album's most baffling aspects – one which 'Darklands' epitomised. It is easy to borrow melodic ideas from other writers, and then shift the chords around until the two tunes are different enough to avoid a plagiarism suit. The Mary Chain were as ready as anyone to wear influences on their sleeve; and they went a stage further, inviting listeners to guess the inspiration. On 'Darklands', it was David Bowie's 'Heroes'; the verses for the two songs fit exactly – try it and see.

'Deep One Perfect Morning' was one of the album's lesser moments, an attempt to duplicate the mood of the singles that came off at half-cock. Once again, the lyrics hinted at deep and secret pain, without ever quite expressing themselves. Only Jim Reid's strangely country-tinged vocal (Johnny Cash on quaaludes?) and the Velvets-inspired tambourine gave the song any individuality.

'Happy When It Rains', presented in identical form to the 12" single version, heightened the pace, and the power, a little. But the side's only uptempo piece was 'Down On Me', in which paranoia, angst and sexual frustration were thrown into the melting pot of a Buzzcocks-style pop song, and then distorted by some buzzsaw guitar.

"There's a couple of things on the LP that are very Rolling Stones-ish," commented William when the record appeared, "like 'Nine Million Rainy Days'; but basically that was tongue-in-cheek at the time. We listened back to it and it sounded great, so we kept it in. But I don't see anything wrong with that; we are essentially fans of rock music, we make music but we're huge fans. I'm a huge fan of that era of The Rolling Stones." More specifically, 'that era' was 'Beggars Banquet', and the backing vocals that woo-hooed across the latter half of 'Nine Million Rainy Days' were reminiscent of The Stones' similar embellishment on their seminal 'Sympathy For The Devil'.

But the song, the second with William at the helm, had more to offer than that. Romance was at stake once again – or rather William was at the stake of romance: 'I'm being dragged from here to hell/And all my time in hell/Is spent with you.' Over a slow, pulsing beat, surrounded by cascades of cymbals and a subliminal buzzing guitar, William offered up an ethereal, almost passionless vocal, like a male Nico, or a neutered Jim Morrison. The effect was startling, disturbing, eerie – a true evocation of the darklands.

'April Skies' opened the second side of 'Darklands', again in extended 12″ form. Then came 'Fall', an obvious tribute to The Stooges, with Jim Reid summoning up the ghost of 'Gimme Danger' era Iggy Pop. Like that band's finest work, this song kept simple – a repetitive three-chord riff with occasional twists, underpinned by a strummed acoustic guitar. The Mary Chain left the complications to the lyrics, which ranged from the sublime ('Hand held holy lust/Dragging me to her cross') to the ridiculous ('Everybody's falling on me/And I'm as dead as a Christmas tree').

The Beach Boys provided the blueprint for 'Cherry Came Too', another of The Mary Chain's exercises in musical shoplifting. This was standard fare; a sixties flavour, the archetypal J&MC tune, and lyrics that delivered the expected link between sex and violence. If Cherry came too, then she probably made someone suffer for it. And the 'Do It Again' chorus suggested that the game wasn't over.

William's final solo track was the most unnerving of all. 'On The Wall' opened with the same descending bass riff as Lou Reed's 'Walk On The Wild Side', and its atmosphere was just as bizarre as that song's gallery of sexual outlaws. Psychoanalysts would have a field day with these lyrics, and their *motifs* of frigidity and despair.

'About You' brought 'Darklands' to a surprising conclusion. The rain is still pouring, but Jim Reid is going to walk on the bright side: 'There's something warm in everything/I know there's something good about you.' And the music had emotion to match, from the nicely-out-of-tune acoustic guitar to Jim's gentle, sensuous vocal.

On first hearing, and for some time thereafter, 'Darklands' was strangely frustrating. It had none of the cathartic surge of 'Psychocandy', or the sleazy atmosphere of 'Some Candy Talking'. With few exceptions, it was a single-paced album, and that pace was slow. A band who once signified liberation – from constraints, from good taste, from the barriers of distortion – were now holding themselves back, like a calm before a storm. Casual listeners were disappointed, even bored.

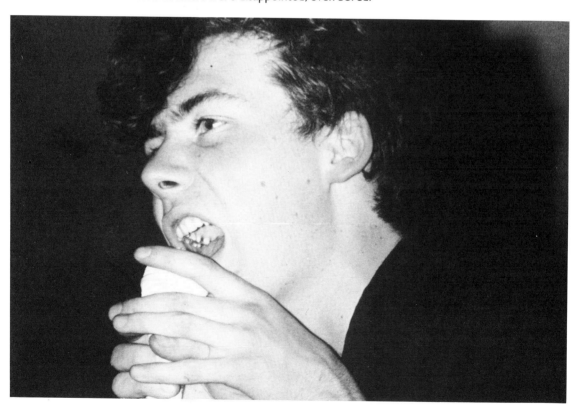

Yet the album is as much a success, on its own terms, as 'Psychocandy'. Without altering their vision, or compromising their principles, The Mary Chain made a record that was utterly different from their first, at a time when straight repetition would have assured underground success. 'Darklands' is not easy listening, but then neither was 'Psychocandy'. Both albums challenged assumptions; it's just that the second album also had to challenge the assumptions of the first.

Guess I'm Dumb

▶

CHAPTER 13

Early in November the band issued the title track of 'Darklands' as another single. Even before the record was released, they had run into trouble. Offered the chance to appear on *The Roxy*, independent TV's stale answer to the equally rancid *Top Of The Pops*, the band had turned up for rehearsal, and put the minimum of effort into the all-important dummy run for the camera. *Roxy* producer Alistair Pirrie was appalled; the new pop ethos was to care, and to care passionately. "We are a chart show which hopefully puts on good acts who perform," he spluttered. "The Mary Chain didn't perform at all. On a scale of one to 10 they didn't register." Faced with hoodlums with no respect for normal show business conventions, the network threw The Mary Chain off the show. Being a Rebel Without A Cause was never so easy.

When it came to marketing, the band weren't quite so revolutionary – either that, or they had no control over their record company. Warner Brothers took saturation marketing to unhealthy extremes with the 'Darklands' single, issuing at least five different configurations of the record. Quite what this has to do with artistic integrity is uncertain. The Mary Chain's principles evidently don't stretch as far as their fans' wallets.

Compact disc owners had already been able to sample the sonic assault of The Mary Chain in digital sound when 'Psychocandy' had belatedly been issued on CD in January 1987 – with, collectors please note, the addition of the otherwise non-LP 'Some Candy Talking'. 'Darklands' appeared simultaneously on LP and CD. Now the 'Darklands' EP appeared as a compact disc single, in a sleeve that was almost identical to the full-length CD. Tower Records of Piccadilly Circus were certainly confused; they continued to offer the CD single at £11.99 (instead of the more usual £4-£5) for several months after it had vanished from every other retail outlet.

The CD single featured an identical track listing to a 10″ single issued at the same time. Alongside 'Darklands' was 'Rider', a song on a familiar subject, as Jim Reid explained: "It's kinda tongue-in-cheek, really. It's us trying to do our old motorbike thing." The song featured the usual grungy guitar, plus an ear-piercing solo that came straight from a Velvets record; but rather than raid their collection of sixties hot rod melodies, the Reids took this model from The Pistols songbook.

On the other side of the 10″ sat two experiments. One was the original demo version of William's 'On The Wall', with guitars that chimed like vibes and gave the piece an oriental sound. Then there was 'Here It Comes Again'. Explained Jim: "Ideally we'd like to experiment with dance music and synthesisers, drum machines and that sort of stuff. Again, there's an ideal dance sound that nobody is doing – based on Hi-NRG stuff that most people would call trashy, like Divine and that. There's actually a song on one of the versions of the single which has got that dance-synth thing. We started off trying it but . . . "It's crap," interjected his brother. Jim went further: "It kinda failed halfway through so we ended up going back to our old style. It failed at what it was trying to do, but it's still good." Well, maybe; it was certainly interesting.

The 7" single included 'Rider' on the flipside; then there were two 12"s, with identical track listings: one simply had a gatefold sleeve, with the 'Darklands' lyrics printed inside for anyone who hadn't yet bought the album. 'Rider' and 'On The Wall' reappeared here – along with a new track. This was a cover of The Beach Boys' 'Surfin' USA', obviously a leftover from the 'Kill Surf City' sessions. 'Kill Surfin' USA' might have been an apter title, as The Mary Chain rode roughshod across the song, mangling it with magnificently off-key feedback solos, and little consideration for its Chuck Berry parentage. And as a glimpse of what might yet be, the Reids ended the song with the voice of a black woman evangelist, presumably taped during one of William's hotel hole-ups in the States.

North America was indeed where the band found themselves in November 1987. On a previous visit, one of their live shows had been taped for use as part of a *Spin* magazine radio transcription. This time the more prestigious Westwood One network recorded a concert in Detroit, broadcasting the show several weeks after the event.

The Mary Chain's appearance at the RPM Club in Toronto was noteworthy for different reasons. A small group of 'fans' heckled the band throughout their set; eventually Jim Reid responded by thrusting his mike stand towards them, striking one person a glancing blow on the head, another a slash across the arm. After the show, the injured parties reported Reid to the local constabulary, who dragged him off the tour bus and into the cells for the night. He was released on bail the next morning, and ordered to return for a court hearing in February.

Come February, a chastened Reid stood up in court to admit his sins – and escaped with an absolute discharge, after he had agreed to donate around £500 to a Salvation Army charity, and apologise to the offended fans. "Everybody, from time to time, behaves stupidly," commented Reid after the case was settled. "Everybody gets drunk, everybody does something that they'd rather not have done, something that, when they wake up the next day, they think, 'Did I do that?' But I suppose if you're in my line of business, if you do it, it's publicly known." And he confirmed that The Mary Chain's hellraising days were over: "This is the last time anything like this happens to me."

The band's reception in mainstream America was scarcely more friendly. They found media coverage difficult to come by, because Americans thought the band's name was blasphemous. It was just as well no-one told the US public anything about the delights of candy. One unlikely American did support the band, however. The freshly slimmed Dolly Parton invited both Reid brothers onto her network TV show, demonstrating either a healthy breadth of musical taste, or some confusion between The Mary Chain and a gospel quartet.

Let Us Go On This Way

▶

CHAPTER 14

The Toronto incident hung over the band during the early months of 1988. Only when Jim Reid was dismissed from the court on probation could they consider the future. For the moment, though, the future was the past, as the band compiled a collection of B-sides and other 'rarities', for mid-price release in April.

As the Reids shovelled through the archives, they hit upon the 'Westwood One' tapes of their Detroit concert in November. Working with producer John Loder, the brothers selected several live tracks for release. In March, 'Nine Million Rainy Days' was given to *Sounds* magazine, for inclusion on the second of their 'Sounds Waves' series of freebie EPs. The live cut demonstrated the increasing strength of the band, with a fury and direction missing from earlier live recordings. The result was like the 1969 Stooges playing Rolling Stones songs, as William Reid's guitar moved Keith Richards' trademark chopping rhythms into fresh arenas. Like the American band, The Divine Horsemen, The Mary Chain were using the late sixties Stones as a stepping stone for sonic experimentation – updating and building on The Stones' innovations rather than imitating them.

Further live tracks emerged in March – as did a various artists compilation dominated by The Mary Chain's contribution. WEA's 'Under The Covers' collected together cover versions from right across their artist roster, with previously released selections by The Pretenders, Everything But The Girl, Brilliant and Fuzzbox. The Mary Chain were represented by 'Surfin' USA', their annihilation of The Beach Boys' classic of summer fun. Their revamp of the Brian Wilson/Chuck Berry tune stood out alongside the likes of Echo And The Bunnymen's gutless cover of The Doors' 'People Are Strange'. While the Bunnymen simply celebrated the sixties as an exercise in pointless nostalgia, The Mary Chain recreated it, thrusting the decade of innocent idealism under the spotlight of eighties realism.

The Mary Chain's own brand of nostalgia reared its head again on the band's new single. 'Sidewalking' was recorded as a try-out, as Jim Reid explained: "It was made in a more relaxed atmosphere than any other record we've ever made. We had no intention of releasing the thing, it's just that, the further we went with it, the better it sounded. It only really became a record that we agreed was gonna be released towards the last mixes, when we were thinking, 'Well, obviously this is too good not to release'."

Everyone who heard the record was struck by one comparison – with Marc Bolan. During the early seventies, the former psychedelic boppin' elf had led T. Rex, who pioneered the return of pure pop that climaxed in the ambiguity of glam-rock. At a time when serious art was the aim of every young musician, Bolan gave music back to the kids, inspiring hysterical scenes in concert and at airports, and rousing the hackles of every elderly critic who thought that pop had finally come of age.

The Mary Chain borrowed Bolan's chugalug guitar rhythms, while Jim Reid forced his voice into an imitation of Marc's insinuating nasal whine. With a tune that nagged at the same three notes throughout, 'Sidewalking' was nothing less than a remake of 'Telegram Sam', though with a definite Mary Chain attitude. And, as usual, William Reid turned the studio into a playground, sweeping from power chords into feedback at the touch of a volume control. He even included a few booming notes of Duane Eddy pastiche to prove he wasn't taking anything too seriously.

Ever willing to proclaim their originality, the Reids denied any Bolan inspiration. "It's not really that obvious," pleaded Jim. "People have said it, but it never occurred to us until after it was recorded. It's quite weird – I can see what people mean, but it wasn't intentional." And he set out on his own revision of critical attitudes: "I think people have been saying it just sounds like a T. Rex record, meaning it's got that same spirit, same atmosphere as the best of the T. Rex records. That could only be a compliment." Indeed. The fact remains, though, that 'Sidewalking' is a blatant Bolan soundalike, at least in seven-inch form. It is also one of the crispest, most commercial Mary Chain singles to date, which deserved far more than its peak chart position just outside the Top Thirty.

If it's the Mary Chain, it must be multiple releases; and the 7″ and 12″ singles were quickly joined by the band's second mini-CD. 12″ and CD alike featured an eight-minute retread of 'Sidewalking', which allowed William Reid more room to play with his feedback, as if to prove the band hadn't lost their ability to frighten. On the CD, there was a third version of 'Sidewalking', this one 'Chilled To The Bone'. Despite its title, version three wasn't a hip-hop remix – it was more radical than that, reducing the steady rhythm of the single to a haze of guitar whine.

And then there were the live tracks – 'Taste Of Cindy' on the 7″, 'Darklands' on the 12″. Both confirmed the band's new-found elegance on stage, without suggesting that a Mary Chain live album was required.

No live double album, then – instead we got the other standard 'holding operation while artist tries to write new songs', the compilation album. 'Barbed Wire Kisses (B-Sides And More)' was actually a useful exercise for everyone who hadn't kept pace with the band's collector's items. The album included flipsides and 12″ bonus tracks galore – 'Kill Surf City', 'Head', 'Rider', 'Hit', 'Just Out Of Reach', 'Happy Place', 'Psycho Candy', 'Who Do You Love', 'Surfin' USA', 'Everything's Alright When You're Down', 'Taste Of Cindy (demo)' and 'On The Wall (demo)'. The cassette and CD releases boasted an extra four cuts: 'Bo Diddley Is Jesus', 'Mushroom', 'Cracked' and 'Here It Comes Again'. Completing the set were the band's previously uncollected first single, 'Upside Down', and two unissued out-takes from the 'Darklands' sessions.

Both of these lacked the finished sheen of the 'Darklands' album, either because they hadn't been remixed as many times, or because they were demos. 'Don't Ever Change' wasn't the old Goffin/King hit for The Crickets, but a Reid/Reid rewrite of their own 'Everything's Alright When You're Down', gentler and comparatively unfocused. 'Swing', meanwhile, lurched between the two-chord swagger of the verse, and the sheer majesty of William's epic guitar solo. And the lyrics gave rise to further speculation about the brothers' bedroom antics: "I wish you and me could be inside of a rubber dream."

The album was meant to be mid-price, though WEA's half-hearted recommendation on the front cover sticker ("Expect to pay as little as possible") left unscrupulous dealers open to naming their own price ticket. The value of 'Barbed Wire Kisses' to collectors was undermined by its almost total lack of annotation; while casual buyers would have found an album that included all the essential ingredients of the J&MC's sound except one – good tunes.

'Barbed Wire Kisses' leaves the band's career neatly in mid-air. The Reids are conscious of their need to avoid pure nostalgia. "I think it's important to sound as if you're making records in 1988," says Jim. "When I hear a record that's a rehash of a sixties thing or something like that, I get a depressing vibe from it. I find it quite depressing that people can bury their heads in the sixties or seventies or fifties or whatever." But The Mary Chain equally have to beware the most common band-trap of

this decade – the endless repetition of a single sound, turning one minor innovation into a career. Potentially major acts like The Fall and Throbbing Gristle plunged over this precipice, establishing a sound and then sticking to it almost neurotically, for fear of alienating any of their equally pigeon-holed supporters.

The Mary Chain have already shown their willingness to move; the shift from the brimstone rhetoric of 'Upside Down' to the languorous misery of 'Darklands' required an act of faith from musicians and fans alike. And 'Sidewalking' represents another modest step away from what the public expects from the band. The dilemma for The Mary Chain is to keep their identity intact while moving their field of vision. Their success will determine whether they will go down in the history books as a great major band or a great minor one.

The fragmentation of the modern rock audience limits the band's possibilities. To change more than a slice of the world, they will have to score hit records; to score hit records, they will have to change their attitudes. Or maybe there is still a thin dividing line between art and commerce, between the avant-garde and appearing on *Wogan*. Time alone will tell.

It is a course The Mary Chain must sail alone. "We always had this idea that lots of groups would start after us and they'd all be brilliant," Jim reflected in 1987. "Instead there's half-a-dozen groups who've come along and sound like we did two years ago, except not as good." The Reids hoped for inspiration, not imitation, but they chose the wrong decade.

What may decide The Mary Chain's fate is the psyche of the brothers Reid. There has been no hint of personal conflict between them; to a remarkable degree, they share a joint vision. The rest of the group is unimportant: bassist Douglas Hart has been indulging his artistic inclinations as producer of Jesse Garon And The Desperados, but if he left The Mary Chain few outsiders would notice. Jim and William Reid are The Mary Chain as much as Marc Bolan was T. Rex. The only threat to their future comes from their own exhaustion.

"I'd like to make four or five albums and have enough to say, 'Right, that's it.' If we could have just one massive-selling LP I would quit. I hate this business. I'd like to just write songs but there's always the feeling now that everything you do is part of your job. Every piece of art or film that you look at, every record you listen to, is going to inspire all your lyrics and music. It's a pretty horrible feeling."
(William Reid, August 1987)

Look ahead a decade. Jim and William Reid are living in a mansion outside Los Angeles, surrounded by guard dogs, barbed wire and machine gun posts. Outside, the world slumbers on; inside the brothers dream of world domination, and dread the human contact it requires. Option One – Phil Spector.

Think again. In a small London club, the compère announces: "The Jesus And Mary Chain." To the embarrassed catcalls of leather-clad 35-year-olds, the Reids carry their paunches onto a greasy, gob-stained stage, and try to conjure up the spirit of rebellion from tired hands and minds. Attempting danger, they achieve comedy. Option Two – Gary Glitter.

And there is a third option, though no-one has yet figured it out. It involves staying one step ahead of the game, knowing when to rest, knowing which opposition represents a threat, which a dead end. In this game-plan, The Mary Chain continue to shock – and to grow. And with a heady mix of rebellion, artistry and luck, they steer the course of mainstream rock away from the marketplace, and back towards the edgy excitement of the cliff edge. The potential is there; all it requires is courage, strength and the will to survive. Option Three – The Jesus And Mary Chain.

Singles

Creation 012
UPSIDE DOWN/VEGETABLE MAN
(October 1984)

Blanco Y Negro NEG 8
NEVER UNDERSTAND/SUCK (February 1985)

Blanco Y Negro NEG 8T
NEVER UNDERSTAND/SUCK/AMBITION
(12", February 1985)

Blanco Y Negro NEG 13
YOU TRIP ME UP/JUST OUT OF REACH
(May 1985)

Blanco Y Negro NEG 13T
YOU TRIP ME UP/JUST OUT OF REACH/
BOYFRIEND'S DEAD (12", May 1985)

Creation 012T
UPSIDE DOWN/VEGETABLE MAN/JESUS
SUCK (12"; release cancelled)

Blanco Y Negro NEG 17
JUST LIKE HONEY/HEAD (September 1985)

Blanco Y Negro NEG 17T
JUST LIKE HONEY/HEAD/CRACKED/JUST
LIKE HONEY (demo) (12", Sept. 1985)

Blanco Y Negro NEG 17F
JUST LIKE HONEY/HEAD/INSIDE ME/JUST
LIKE HONEY (demo) (double-pack single,
September 1985)

Blanco Y Negro NEG 19
SOME CANDY TALKING/
PSYCHOCANDY/HIT (July 1986)

Blanco Y Negro NEG 19T
SOME CANDY TALKING/
PSYCHOCANDY/HIT/TASTE OF CINDY
(acoustic) (12", July 1986)

Blanco Y Negro NEG 19F
SOME CANDY TALKING/
PSYCHOCANDY/HIT/CUT DEAD
(acoustic)/PSYCHOCANDY (acoustic)/
YOU TRIP ME UP (acoustic)/SOME
CANDY TALKING (acoustic) (double-pack
single, July 1986)

Blanco Y Negro NEG 24
APRIL SKIES/KILL SURF CITY (April 1987)

Blanco Y Negro NEG 24T
APRIL SKIES (long version)/KILL SURF
CITY/WHO DO YOU LOVE (12",
April 1987)

Blanco Y Negro NEG 24F
APRIL SKIES/KILL SURF CITY/
MUSHROOM (live in Nuremburg 1986)/BO
DIDDLEY IS JESUS (double-pack single,
April 1987)

Blanco Y Negro NEG 25
HAPPY WHEN IT RAINS/EVERYTHING'S
ALRIGHT WHEN YOU'RE DOWN (August
1987)

Blanco Y Negro NEG 25T
HAPPY WHEN IT RAINS (long version)/
EVERYTHING'S ALRIGHT WHEN YOU'RE
DOWN/HAPPY PLACE/F-HOLE (12",
August 1987)

Blanco Y Negro NEG 25E
HAPPY WHEN IT RAINS/EVERYTHING'S
ALRIGHT WHEN YOU'RE DOWN/
SHAKE/HAPPY WHEN IT RAINS (demo)
(10", August 1987)

Blanco Y Negro NEG 25B
HAPPY WHEN IT RAINS (long version)/
SHAKE/EVERYTHING'S ALRIGHT WHEN
YOU'RE DOWN (7" single in box with
postcards, August 1987)

Blanco Y Negro NEG 29
DARKLANDS/RIDER/ON THE WALL
(porta studio demo) (November 1987)

Blanco Y Negro NEG 29T
DARKLANDS/RIDER/SURFIN' USA (April
out-take)/ON THE WALL (porta studio
demo) (12", initially in gatefold sleeve,
November 1987)

Blanco Y Negro NEG 29E
DARKLANDS/RIDER/HERE IT COMES
AGAIN/ON THE WALL (porta studio
demo) (10", November 1987)

Blanco Y Negro NEG 29CD
DARKLANDS/RIDER/HERE IT COMES
AGAIN/ON THE WALL (porta studio
demo) (CD single, November 1987)

Blanco Y Negro NEG 32
SIDEWALKING/TASTE OF CINDY (live in
Detroit) (March 1988)

Blanco Y Negro NEG 32T
SIDEWALKING (extended)/TASTE OF
CINDY (live in Detroit)/DARKLANDS
(live in Detroit)/SIDEWALKING (12",
March 1988)

Blanco Y Negro NEG 32CD
SIDEWALKING/SIDEWALKING
(extended)/TASTE OF CINDY (live in
Detroit)/SIDEWALKING (Chilled to the
Bone) (CD single, March 1988)

Albums

Blanco Y Negro BYN 7
PSYCHOCANDY (November 1985)
Side One: JUST LIKE HONEY/THE LIVING
END/TASTE THE FLOOR/THE HARDEST
WALK/CUT DEAD/IN A HOLE/TASTE C
CINDY
Side Two: NEVER UNDERSTAND/INSIDE
ME/SOWING SEEDS/MY LITTLE
UNDERGROUND/YOU TRIP ME UP/
SOMETHING'S WRONG/IT'S SO HARD
CD release has one extra track: SOME
CANDY TALKING

Baktabak BAK 2034
THE JESUS AND MARY CHAIN (August
1987; picture disc)
Side One: Interview with Jim & William Reic
Side Two: Interview with Jim & William Rei
(part 2)

Various EP's

The Hit HOT 001
THE HIT RED HOT EP (1985; includes
TASTE OF CINDY)

NME GIV 3
NME'S BIG FOUR (1986; includes SOME
CANDY TALKING)

Sounds WAVES 2
SOUNDS WAVES 2 (1988; includes NINE
MILLION RAINY DAYS (live in Detroit)